The Art of Poetry volume

Edexcel IGCSE

With thanks to Matthew Curry, Johanna Harrison and Kathrine Mortimore.

And to my family for letting me hide away and keep writing.

Published by Peripeteia Press Ltd.

First published June 2017

ISBN: 978-0-9954671-8-7

Peripeteia.webs.com

Contents

General Introduction to the The Art of Poetry series

The philosopher Nietzsche described his work as 'the greatest gift that [mankind] has ever been given'. The Elizabethan poet Edmund Spenser hoped his epic, *The Faerie Queene,* would magically transform its readers into noblemen. In comparison, our aims for *The Art of Poetry* series of books are a little more modest. Fundamentally we aim to provide books that will be of maximum use to English students and their teachers. In our experience, few students read essays on poems, yet, whatever specification they are studying, they have to write analytical essays on poetry. So, we've offering some models, written in a lively, accessible and, we hope, engaging style. We believe that the essay as a form needs demonstrating and championing, especially as so many revision books for students present information in broken down note form.

For Volume 1 we chose canonical poems for several reasons: Firstly, they are simply great poems, well worth reading and studying; secondly, we chose poems from across time so that they sketch in outline major developments in English poetry, from the Elizabethan period up until the present day, so that the volume works as an introduction to poetry and poetry criticism. Our popular volumes 2-5 focused on poems set at A-level by the Edexcel and AQA boards respectively. Volumes 6 to 11 tackled GCSE anthologies from AQA, Eduqas, OCR and Edexcel. In this current volume, we our focus turns for the first time to IGCSE, providing critical support for students reading poems from Edexcel's new IGCSE poetry anthology. In particular, we hope our book will help and inspire those students aiming to reach the very highest numerical grades, 7-9.

How to analyse a poem [seen or unseen]

A list of ingredients, not a recipe

Firstly, what not to do: sometimes pupils have been so programmed to spot poetic features such as alliteration that they start analysis of a poem with close reading of these micro aspects of technique. This is never a clever idea. A far better strategy is to begin by trying to develop an overall understanding of what you think the poem is about. While, obviously, all these poems are about relationships of some sort or other, the nature of these relationships vary widely what they have say about this topic is also highly varied. Once you've established the central concerns, you can delve into the poem's interior, examining its inner workings in the light of these. And you should be flexible enough to adapt, refine or even reject your initial thoughts in the light of your investigation. The essential thing is to make sure that whether you're discussing imagery or stanza form, sonic effects or syntax, enjambment or vocabulary, you always explore the significance of the feature in terms of meanings and effect.

Someone once compared texts to cakes. When you're presented with a cake the first thing you notice is what it looks like. Probably the next thing you'll do is taste it and find out if you like the flavour. This aesthetic experience will come first. Only later might you investigate the ingredients and how it was made. Adopting a uniform reading strategy is like a recipe; it sets out what you must, do step by step, in a predetermined order. This can be helpful, especially when you start reading and analysing poems. Hence in our first volume in *The Art of Poetry* series we explored each poem under the same subheadings of narrator, characters, imagery, patterns of sound, form & structure and contexts, and all our essays followed essentially the same direction. Of course, this is a reasonable strategy for reading poetry and will stand you in good stead. However, this present volume takes a different, more flexible approach, because this book is designed for students aiming for levels 7 to 9, or A to A* in old currency, and to reach the highest levels your work needs to be a bit more conceptual, critical and individual. Writing frames are useful for beginners, like stabilisers when you learn to ride a bike. But, if you wish to write top level essays you need to develop your own frames.

Read our essays and you'll find that they all include the same principle ingredients – detailed, 'fine-grained' reading of crucial elements of poetry, imagery, form, rhyme and so forth - but each essay starts in a different way and each one has a slightly different focus or weight of attention on the various aspects that make up a poem. Once you feel you have mastered the apprentice strategy of reading all poems in the same way, we strongly recommend you put this generic essay recipe approach to one side and move on to a new way of reading, an approach that can change depending on the nature of the poem you're reading.

Follow your nose
Having established what you think a poem is about - its theme and what is interesting about the poet's treatment of the theme [the conceptual bit] - rather than then working through a pre-set agenda, decide what you honestly think are the most interesting aspects of the poem and start analysing these closely. This way your response will be original [a key marker of a top band essay] and you'll be writing about material you find most interesting. In other words, you're foregrounding yourself as an individual, critical reader. These most interesting aspects might be ideas or technique based, or both.

Follow your own, informed instincts, trust in your own critical intelligence as a reader. If you're writing about material that genuinely interests you, your writing is likely to be interesting for the examiner too. And, obviously, take advice to from your teacher too, use their expertise.

Because of the focus on sonic effects and imagery other aspects of poems are often overlooked by students. It is a rare student, for instance, who notices how punctuation works in a poem and who can write about it convincingly. Few students write about the contribution of the unshowy function words, such as pronouns, prepositions or conjunctions, yet these words are crucial to any text. Of course, it would be a highly risky strategy to focus your whole essay on a seemingly innocuous and incidental detail of a poem. But coming at things from an unusual angle is as important to writing great essays as it is to the production of great poetry.

So, in summary, when reading a poem for the first time, such as when doing an 'unseen' style question, have a check list in mind, but don't feel you must follow someone else's generic essay recipe. Don't feel that you must always start with a consideration of imagery if the poem you're analysing has, for instance, an eye-catching form. Consider the significance of major features, such as imagery, vocabulary, sonic patterns and form. Try to write about these aspects in terms of their contribution to themes and effects. But also follow your nose, find your own direction, seek out aspects that genuinely engage you and write about these.

The essays in this volume provide examples and we hope they will encourage you to go your own way, at least to some extent, and to make discoveries for yourself. No single essay could possibly cover everything that could be said about any one of these poems; aiming to create comprehensive essays like this would be utterly foolish. And we have not tried to do so. Nor are our essays meant to be models for exam essays – they're far too long for that. They do, however, illustrate the sort of conceptualised, critical and 'fine-grained' exploration demanded for top grades at GCSE and beyond. There's always more to be discovered, more to say, space in other words for you to develop some original reading of your own, space for you to write your own individual essay recipe.

Writing Literature essays

The Big picture and the small

An essay itself can be a form of art. And writing a great essay takes time, skill and practice. And also expert advice. Study the two figures in the picture carefully and describe what you can see. Channel your inner Sherlock Holmes to add any deductions you are able to form about the image. Before reading what we have to say, write your description out as a prose paragraph. Probably you'll have written something along the following lines:

First off, the overall impression: this picture is very blurry. Probably this indicates that either this is a very poor quality reproduction, or that it is a copy of a very small detail from a much bigger image that has been magnified several times. The image shows a stocky man and a medium-sized dog, both orientated towards something to their left, which suggests there is some point of interest in that direction. From the man's rustic dress (smock, breeches, clog-like boots) the picture is either an old one or a modern one depicting the past. The man appears to be carrying a stick and there's maybe a bag on his back. From all of these details we can probably deduce that he's a peasant, maybe a farmer or a shepherd.

 Now do the same thing for picture two. We have even less detail here and again the picture's blurry. Particularly without the benefit of colour it's hard to determine what we're seeing other than a horizon and maybe the sky. We might just be able to make out that in the centre of the picture is the shape of the sun. From the reflection, we can deduce that the image is of the sun either setting or rising over water. If it is dawn this usually symbolises hope, birth and new beginnings; if the sun is setting it conventionally symbolises the opposite – the end of things, the coming of

night/ darkness, death.

If you're a sophisticated reader, you might well start to think about links between the two images. Are they, perhaps, both details from the same single larger image, for instance.

Well, this image might be even harder to work out. Now we don't even have a

whole figure, just a leg, maybe, sticking up in the air. Whatever is happening here, it looks painful and we can't even see the top half of the body. From the upside orientation, we might guess that the figure is or has fallen. If we put this image with the one above, we might think the figure has fallen into water as there are horizontal marks on the image that could be splashes. From the quality of this image we can deduce that this is an even smaller detail blown-up.

You may be wondering by now why we've suddenly moved into rudimentary art appreciation. On the other hand, you may already have worked out the

point of this exercise. Either way, bear with us, because this is the last picture for you to describe and analyse. So, what have we here? Looks like another peasant, again from the past, perhaps medieval (?) from the smock-like dress, clog-like shoes and the britches. This character is also probably male and seems to be pushing some wooden apparatus from left to right. From the ridges at the bottom left of the image we can surmise that he's working the land, probably driving a plough. Noticeably the figure has his back to us;

we see his turned away from us, suggesting his whole concentration is on the task at hand. In the background appear to be sheep, which would fit with our impression that this is an image of farming. It seems likely that this image and the first one come from the same painting. They have a similar style and subject and it is possible that these sheep belong to our first character. This image is far less blurry than the other one. Either it is a better-quality reproduction, or this is a larger, more significant detail extracted from the original source. If this is a significant detail it's interesting that we cannot see the character's face. From this we can deduce that he's not important in and of himself; rather he's a representative figure and the important thing is what he is and what he isn't looking at.

Okay, we hope we haven't stretched your patience too far. What's the point of all this? Well, let's imagine we prefixed the paragraphs above with an introduction, along the following lines: 'The painter makes this picture interesting and powerful by using several key techniques and details' and that we added a conclusion, along the lines of 'So now I have shown how the painter has made this picture interesting and powerful through the use of a number of key techniques and details'. Finally, substitute painter and picture for writer and text. If we put together our paragraphs into an essay what would be its strengths and weaknesses? What might be a better way of writing our essay?

Consider the strengths first off. The best bits of our essay, we humbly suggest, are the bits where we begin to explain what we are seeing, when we do the Holmes like deductive thinking. Another strength might be that we have started to make links between the various images, or parts of a larger image, to see how they work together to provide us more information. A corresponding weakness is that each of our paragraphs seems like a separate chunk of writing. The weaker parts of the paragraphs are where we simply describe what we can see. More importantly though, if we used our comments on image one as our first paragraph we seem to have started in a rather random way. Why should we have begun our essay with that image? What was the logic behind that? And most importantly of all, if this image is an analogue for a specific aspect of a text, such as a poem's imagery or a novel's dialogue we have dived straight into to analysing this technical aspect before we're established any overall sense of the painting/ text. And this is a very common fault with GCSE English Literature essays. As we've said before and will keep saying, pupils start writing detailed micro-analysis of a detail such as alliteration before they have established the big picture of what the text is about and what the answer to the question they've been set might be. Without this big picture it's very difficult to write about the significance of the micro details. And the major marks for English essays are reserved for explanations of the significance and effects generated by a writer's craft.

Now we'll try a different and much better approach. Let's start off with the big picture, the whole image. The painting on the next page is called *Landscape with the fall of Icarus*. It's usually attributed to the Renaissance artist, Pieter Breughel and was probably painted in the 1560s. Icarus is a character from

 Greek mythology. He was the son of the brilliant inventor, Daedalus. Trapped on Crete by the evil King Minos, Daedalus and Icarus managed to escape when the inventor created pairs of giant feathered wings. Before they took to sky Daedalus warned his son not to get too excited and fly too near the sun as the wings were held together by wax that might melt. Icarus didn't listen, however. The eventual result was that he plummeted back to earth, into the sea more precisely and was killed.

Applying this contextual knowledge to the painting we can see that the image is about how marginal Icarus' tragedy is in the big picture. Conventionally we'd expect any image depicting such a famous myth to make Icarus's fall the dramatic centre of attention. The main objects of this painting, however, are emphatically not the falling boy hitting the water. Instead our eye is drawn to the peasant in the centre of the painting, pushing his plough (even more so in colour as his shirt is the only red object in an otherwise greeny-yellow landscape) and the stately galleon sailing calmly past those protruding legs. Seeing the whole image, we can appreciate the significance of the shepherd and the ploughman looking up and down and to the left. The point being made is how they don't even notice the tragedy because they have work to do and need to get on with their lives. The animals too seem unconcerned. As W. H. Auden puts it, in lines from *Musée des Beaux Arts*, 'everything turns away /

Quite leisurely from the disaster'.

To sum up, when writing an essay on any literary text do not begin with close-up analysis of micro-details. Begin instead with establishing the whole picture: What the text is about, what key techniques the writer uses, when it was written, what sort of text it is, what effects it has on the reader. Then, when you zoom in to examine smaller details, such as imagery, individual words, metre or sonic techniques you can discuss these in relation to their significance in terms of this bigger picture.

What would our art appreciation essay look like now?

Paragraph #1: Introduction – myth of Icarus, date of painting, the way our eyes is drawn away from his tragic death to much more ordinary life going around him. Significance of this – even tragic suffering goes on around us without us even noticing, we're too busy getting on with our lives.

Paragraph #2: We could, of course, start with our first figure and follow the same order as we've presented the images here. But wouldn't it make more logical sense to discuss first the biggest, more prominent images in the painting first? So, our first paragraph is about the ploughman and his horse. How his figure placed centrally and is bent downwards towards the ground and turned left away from us etc.

Paragraph #3: The next most prominent image is the ship. Also moving from right to left, as if the main point of interest in the painting is off in that direction. Here we could consider the other human agricultural figure, the shepherd and his dog and, of course, the equally oblivious sheep.

Paragraph #4: Having moved on to examining background details in the painting we could discuss the symbolism of the sun on the horizon. While this could be the sun rising, the context of the story suggests it is more likely to be setting. The pun of the sun/son going down makes sense.

Paragraph #5: Finally, we can turn our attention to the major historical and literary figure in this painting, Icarus and how he is presented. This is the key image in terms of understanding the painting's purpose and effect.

Paragraph #6: Conclusion. What is surprising about this picture. How do the choices the painter makes affect us as viewer/ reader? Does this painting make Icarus's story seem more pathetic, more tragic or something else?

Now, all you have to do is switch from a painting to a poem.

Big pictures, big cakes, recipes and lists of instructions; following your own nose and going your own way. Whatever metaphors we use, your task is to bring something personal and individual to your critical reading of poems and to your essay writing.

Writing comparative essays

The following is adapted from our discussion of this topic in *The Art of Writing English Literature Essay*s A-level course companion, and is a briefer version, tailored to the GCSE exam task. Fundamentally comparative essays want you to display not only your ability to intelligently talk about literary texts, but also your ability to make meaningful connections between them. The first starting point is your topic. This must be broad enough to allow substantial thematic overlapping of the texts. However, too little overlap and it will be difficult to connect the texts; too much overlap and your discussion will be lopsided and one-dimensional. In the case of the Edexcel IGCSE the exam question will ask you to focus on the methods used by the poets to explore how two poems present one of these themes. You will also be directed to write specifically on language and imagery [AO2].

You will have the choice of two questions on the poetry anthology. On the first, two poems will be chosen for you; on the second question you will be given one poem from the anthology and you will then have to choose a companion poem. Selecting the right poem for interesting comparison is obviously very important. Obviously, you should prepare for this question beforehand by pairing up the poems, especially as you will only have about forty minutes to complete this task.

To think about this task visually, you don't want Option A, below, [not enough overlap] or Option B [two much overlap]. You want Option C. This option allows substantial common links to be built between your chosen texts where discussion arises from both fundamental similarities AND differences.

Option A: too many differences

Option B: too many similarities

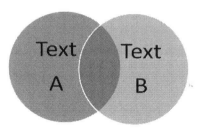

Option C: suitable number of similarities and differences

The final option will generate the most interesting discussion as it will allow substantial similarities to emerge as well as differences. <u>The best comparative essays actually find that what seemed like clear similarities become subtle differences and vice versa</u> while still managing to find rock solid similarities to build their foundations on.

Check the mark scheme for this question and you'll notice that to reach the top grade your comparison must be 'well-structured'. How should you structure a comparative essay? Consider the following alternatives. Which one is best and why?

Essay Structure #1

1. Introduction
2. Main body paragraph #1 - Text A
3. Main body paragraph #2 - Text A
4. Main body paragraph #3 - Text B
5. Main body paragraph #4 - Text B
6. Conclusion

Essay Structure #2

1. Introduction
2. Main body paragraph #1 - Text A
3. Main body paragraph #2 - Text A
4. Main body paragraph #3 - Text B
5. Main body paragraph #4 - Text B
6. Comparison of main body paragraphs #1 & #3 - Text A + B
7. Comparison of main body paragraphs #2 & #4 - Text A + B
8. Conclusion

Essay Structure #3

1. Introduction
2. Main body paragraph #1 - Text A + B
3. Main body paragraph #2 - Text A + B
4. Main body paragraph #3 - Text A + B
5. Main body paragraph #4 - Text A+ B
6. Conclusion

We hope you will agree that 3 is the optimum option. Option 1 is the dreaded 'here is everything I know about text A, followed by everything I know by Text B' approach where the examiner has to work out what the connections are between the texts. This will score the lowest marks. Option 2 is better: There is some attempt to compare the two texts. However, it is a very inefficient way of comparing the two texts. For comparative essay writing the most important thing is to discuss both texts together. This is the most effective and efficient way of achieving your overall aim. Option 3 does this by comparing and contrasting the two texts under common umbrella headings. This naturally encourages comparison. Using comparative discourse markers, such as 'similarly', 'in contrast to', 'conversely' 'likewise' and 'however' also facilitates effective comparison.

When writing about each poem, make sure you do not work chronologically through a poem, summarising the content of each stanza. Responses of this sort typically start with 'In the first stanza' and employ discourse markers of time rather than comparison, such as 'after', 'next', 'then' and so forth. Even if your reading is analytical rather than summative, your essay should not work through the poem from the opening to the ending. Instead, make sure you write about the ideas explored in both texts (themes), the feelings and effects generated and the techniques the poets utilise to achieve these.

Writing about language

Poems are paintings as well as windows; we look at them as well as through them. As you know, special attention should be paid to language in poetry because of all the literary art forms poetry, in particular, employs language in a precise, self-conscious and distinctive way. Ideally in poetry, every word should count. Analysis of language falls into distinct categories:

- By diction we mean the vocabulary used in a poem. A poem might be composed from the ordinary language of everyday speech or it might use elaborate, technical or elevated phrasing. Or both. At one time, some words and types of words were considered inappropriate for the rarefied field of poetry. The great Irish poet, W. B. Yeats never referred to modern technology in his poetry, there are no cars, or tractors or telephones, because he did not consider such things fitting for poetry. When much later, Philip Larkin used swear words in his otherwise well-mannered verse the effect was deeply shocking. Modern poets have pretty much dispensed with the idea of there being an elevated literary language appropriate for poetry. Hence in the IGCSE anthology you'll find all sorts of modern, everyday language.

- Grammatically a poem may use complex or simple sentences [the key to which is the conjunctions]; it might employ a wash of adjectives and adverbs, or it may rely extensively on the bare force of nouns and verbs. Picking out and exploring words from specific grammatical classes has the merit of being both incisive and usually illuminating.

- Poets might mix together different types, conventions and registers of language, moving, for example, between formal and informal, spoken and written, modern and archaic, and so forth. Arranging the diction in the poem in terms of lexico-semantic fields, by register or by etymology, helps reveal underlying patterns of meaning.

- For almost all poems imagery is a crucial aspect of language. Broadly imagery is a synonym for description and can be broken down into two types, sensory and figurative. Sensory imagery means the words and phrases that appeal to our senses, to touch and taste, hearing, smell and sight. Sensory imagery is evocative; it helps to take us into the world of the poem to share the experience being described. Figurative imagery, in particular, is always significant. As we have mentioned, not all poems rely on metaphors and similes; these devices are only part of a poet's box of tricks, but figurative language is always important when it occurs because it compresses multiple meanings into itself. To use a technical term figurative images are polysemic - they contain many meanings. Try writing out the all the meanings contained in a metaphor in a more concise and economical way. Even simple, everyday metaphors compress meaning. If we want to say our teacher is fierce and powerful and that we fear his or her wrath, we can more concisely *say our teacher is a dragon.*

Writing about patterns of sound

Like painters, some poets have powerful visual imaginations, while other poets have stronger auditory imaginations are more like musicians. And some poems are like paintings, others are more like pieces of music.

Firstly, what not to do: Tempting as it may be to spot sonic features of a poem and list these, don't do this. Avoid something along the lines of 'The poet uses alliteration here and the rhyme scheme is ABABCDCDEFEFGG'. Sometimes, indeed, it may be tempting to set out the poem's whole rhyme scheme like this. Resist the temptation: This sort of identification of features is worth zero marks. Marks in exams are reserved for attempts to link techniques to meanings and to effects.

Probably many of us have been sitting in English lessons listening somewhat sceptically as our English teacher explains the surprisingly specific significance of a seemingly random piece of alliteration in a poem. Something along the lines 'The double d sounds here reinforce a sense of invincible strength' or 'the harsh repetition of the 't' sounds suggests anger'. Through all our minds at some point may have passed the idea that, in these instances, English teachers appear to be using some sort of Enigma-style secret symbolic decoding machine that reveals how particular patterns of sounds have such definite encoded meanings.

And this sort of thing is not all nonsense. Originally deriving from an oral tradition, poems are, of course, written for the ear as much as for the eye, to be heard as much as read. A poem is a soundscape as much as it is a set of meanings. Sounds are, however, difficult to tie to very definite meanings and effects. By way of example, the old BBC Radiophonic workshop, which produced ambient sounds for radio and television programmes, used the same sounds in different contexts, knowing that the audience would perceive them in the appropriate way because of that context. Hence the sound of bacon sizzling, of an audience clapping and of feet walking over gravel were actually recordings of an identical sound. Listeners heard them differently because of the context. So, we may, indeed, be able to spot the repeated 's' sounds in a poem, but whether this creates a hissing sound, yes like a snake, or the susurration of the sea will depend on the context within the poem and the ears of the reader. Whether a sound is soft and soothing or harsh and grating is also open to interpretation.

The idea of connecting these sounds to meanings or significance is a productive one. And your analysis will be most convincing if you use several pieces of evidence together. In other words, rather than try to pick out individual examples of sonic effects we recommend you explore 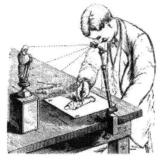 the weave or pattern of sounds, the effects these generate and their contribution to feelings and ideas. For example, this might mean examining how alliteration and assonance are used together to achieve a particular mimetic effect.

Writing about form & structure

As you know, there are no marks for simply identifying textual features. This holds true for language, sounds and also for form. Consider instead the relationship between a poem's form and its content, themes and effects. Form is not merely decorative or ornamental: A poem's meanings and effects are generated through the interplay of form and content. Broadly speaking the form can either work with or against a poem's content. Conventionally a sonnet, for instance, is about love, whereas a limerick is a comic form. A serious love poem in the form of a limerick would be unusual, as would a sonnet about an old man with a beard.

Sometimes poetic form can create an ironic backdrop to highlight an aspect of content. An example would be a formally elegant poem about something

 monstrous, or a fragile form containing something robust or vice versa. Browning's *My Last Duchess* might spring to mind. The artist Grayson Perry uses form in this ironic way. Rather than depicting the sort of picturesque, idealised images we expect of ceramics, Perry's pots and urns depict modern life in bright, garish colours. The urn pictured, for instance, is entitled *Modern Fa*mily and depicts two gay men with a boy who they have presumably adopted. A thrash metal concert inside a church, a philosophical essay via text message, a fine crystal goblet filled with cherryade would be further examples of ironic relationships between message and medium, content and context or form.

****

Reading form
Put a poem before your eyes. Start off taking a panoramic perspective: Think of the forest, not the trees. Perhaps mist over your eyes a bit. Don't even read

the words, just look at the poem, like at a painting. Is the poem slight, thin, fat, long, short? What is the relation of whiteness to blackness? Why might the poet have chosen this shape? Does it look regular or irregular? A poem about a long winding river will probably look rather different from one about a small pebble, or should do. Unless form is being employed ironically. Now read the poem a couple of times. First time, fast as you can, second time more slowly and carefully. How does the visual layout of the poem relate to what it seems to be about? Does this form support, or create a tension against, the content? Is the form one you recognise, like a sonnet, or is it more open, more irregular like free verse? Usually the latter is obvious from the irregularity of the stanzas, line lengths and lack of metre or rhyme.

As Hurley and O'Neill explain in *Poetic Form: An Introduction*, like genre, form sets expectations: 'In choosing form, poets bring into play associations and expectations which they may then satisfy, modify or subvert'.[1] We've already suggested that if we see a poem is a sonnet or a limerick this recognition will set up expectations about the nature of the poem's content. The same thing works on a smaller level; once we have noticed that a poem's first stanza is a quatrain, we expect it to continue in this neat, orderly fashion. If the quatrain's rhyme scheme is xaxa, xbxb, in which only the second and fourth lines rhyme, we reasonably expect that the next stanza will be xcxc. So, if it isn't we need to consider why.

After taking in the big picture in terms of choice of form in relation to content zoom in: Explore the stanza form, lineation, punctuation, the use of enjambment and caesura. Single line stanzas draw attention to themselves. If they are end-stopped they can suggest isolation, separation. Couplets imply twoness. Stanzas of three lines are called tercets and feature in villanelles and terza rima. On the page, both these forms tend to look rather delicate, especially if separated from each other by the silence of white space. Often balanced through rhyme, quatrains look a bit more robust and sturdy. Cinquains are swollen quatrains in which the last line often seems to throw

---

[1] Hurley & O'Neill, *Poetic Form, An Introduction*, p.3

the stanza out of balance.

Focus in on specific examples and on points of transition. For instance, if a poem has four regular quatrains followed by a couplet, examine the effect of this change. If we've been ticking along nicely in iambic metre and suddenly trip on a trochee, examine why. Consider regularity. Closed forms of poems, such as sonnets, are highly regular with set rhyme schemes, metre and number of lines. The opposite form is called 'open', the most extreme version of which is free verse. In free verse poems, the poet dispenses with any set metre, rhyme scheme or recognisable traditional form. What stops this sort of poetry from being prose chopped up to look like verse? The care of the design on the page. Hence, we need to focus here on lineation. Enjambment runs over lines and makes connections; caesura pauses a line and separates words. Lots of enjambment generates a sense of the language running away from the speaker. Lots of caesuras generate a halting, hesitant, choppy movement to lines. Opposites, these devices work in tandem and where they fall is always significant in a good poem.

Remember poetic form is never merely decorative. And bear in mind too the fact that the most volatile materials require the strongest containers.

Nice to metre...
A brief guide to metre and rhythm in poetry

Why express yourself in poetry? Why read words dressed up and expressed as a poem? What can you get from poetry that you can't from prose? There are many compelling answers to these questions. Here, though, we're going to concentrate on one aspect of the unique appeal of poetry – the structure of sound in poetry. Whatever our stage of education, we are all already sophisticated at detecting and using structured sound. Try reading the following sentences without any variation whatsoever in how each sound is  emphasised, and they will quickly lose what essential human characteristics they have. The sentences will sound robotic. So, in a sense, we won't be teaching anything new here. It's just that in poetry the structure of sound is carefully unusually crafted and created. It becomes a key part of what a poem is.

We will introduce a few new key technical terms along the way, but the ideas are straightforward. Individual sounds [syllables] are either stressed [emphasised, sounding louder and longer] or unstressed. As well as clustering into words and sentences for meaning, these sounds [syllables] cluster into rhythmic groups or feet, producing the poem's metre, which is the characteristic way its rhythm works.

In some poems, the rhythm is very regular and may even have a name, such as iambic pentameter. At the other extreme a poem may have no discernible regularity at all. As we have said, this is called free verse. It is vital to remember that the sound in a good poem is structured so that it combines effectively with the meanings.

For example, take a look at these two lines from Marvell's *To his Coy Mistress*:

'But at my back I alwaies hear
Times winged Chariot hurrying near:'

Forgetting the rhythms for a moment, Marvell is basically saying at this point 'Life is short, Time flies, and it's after us'. Now concentrate on the rhythm of his words.

- In the first line every other syllable is stressed: 'at', 'back', 'al', 'hear'.
- Each syllable before these is unstressed 'But', 'my', 'I', 'aies'.
- This is a regular beat or rhythm which we could write
  ti TUM / ti TUM / ti TUM / ti TUM , with the / separating the feet. ['Feet' is the technical term for metrical units of sound]
- This type of two beat metrical pattern is called iambic, and because there are four feet in the line, it is tetrameter. So this line is in 'iambic tetrameter'. [Tetra is Greek for four]
- Notice that 'my' and 'I' being unstressed diminishes the speaker, and we are already prepared for what is at his 'back', what he can 'hear' to be bigger than him, since these sounds are stressed.
- On the next line, the iambic rhythm is immediately broken off, since the next line hits us with two consecutive stressed syllables straight off: 'Times' 'wing'. Because a pattern had been established, when it suddenly changes the reader feels it, the words feel crammed together more urgently, the beats of the rhythm are closer, some little parcels of time have gone missing.

A physical rhythmic sensation is created of time slipping away, running out. This subtle sensation is enhanced by the stress-unstress-unstress pattern of words that follow, 'chariot hurrying' [TUM-ti-ti, TUM-ti-ti]. So the hurrying sounds underscore the meaning of the words.

26

14 ways of looking at a poem

 Though conceived as pre-reading exercises, most of these tasks work just as well for revision.

1. Mash them (1) – mix together lines from two or more poems. The students' task is to untangle the poems from each other.

2. Mash them (2) – the second time round make the task significantly harder. Rather than just mixing whole lines, mash the poems together more thoroughly, words, phrases, images and all, so that unmashing seems impossible. At first sight.

3. Dock the last stanza or few lines from a poem. The students should come up with their own endings for the poem. Compare with the poet's version. Or present the poem without its title. Can the students come up with a suitable one?

4. Break a poem into segments. Split the class into groups. Each group work in isolation on their segment and feedback on what they discover. Then their task is to fit the poem and their ideas about it together as a whole.

5. Give the class the first and last stanza of a poem. Their task is to provide the filling. They can choose to attempt the task at beginner level (in prose) or at world class level (in poetry).

6. Add superfluous words to a poem. Start off with obvious interventions, such as the interjection of blatantly alien, noticeable words. Try smuggling 'pineapple', 'bourbon' and 'haberdashers' into any of the poems and see if you can get it past the critical sensors.

7. Repeat the exercise – This time using much less extravagant words. Try to smuggle in a few intensifiers, such as 'really', 'very' and 'so'. Or extra adjectives.

8. Collapse the lineation in a poem and present it as continuous prose. The students' task is to put it back into verse. Discussing the various pros and cons or various possible arrangements – short lines, long lines, irregular lines - can be very productive. Pay particular attention to line breaks and the words that end them. After a whatever-time-you-deem-fit, give the class the pattern of the first stanza. They then have to decide how to arrange the next stanza. Drip feed the rest of the poem to them.

9. Find a way to present the shapes of each poem on the page without the words. The class should work through each poem, two minutes at a time, speculating on what the shape might tell us about the content of the poem. This exercise works especially well as a starter activity. We recommend you use two poems at a time, as the comparison helps students to recognise and appreciate different shapes.

10. Test the thesis that an astute reader can recognise poems by men from those written by women. Give the class one of the poems, such as *War Photographer* or *Prayer Before Birth*, without the name of the poet. Ask them to identify whether the writer is male or female and to explain their reasons for identifying them as such.

11. Split the class into groups. Each group should focus their analysis on a different feature of the poem. Start with the less obvious aspects: Group 1 should concentrate on enjambment and caesuras; group 2 on punctuation; group 3 on the metre and rhythm; group 4 on function words – conjunctions, articles, prepositions. 2-5 mins. only. Then swap focus, four times. Share findings.

12. In **Observations on Poetry**, Robert Graves wrote that 'rhymes properly used are the good servants whose presence at the dinner-table gives the guests a sense of opulent security; never awkward or over-clever, they hand the dishes silently and professionally. You can trust them not to interrupt the conversation or allow their personal disagreements to come to the notice of the guests; but some of them are getting very old for their work'. Explore the poets' use of rhyme in the light of Graves' comment. Are the rhymes ostentatiously original or old hat? Do they stick out of the poem or are they neatly tucked in? Are they dutiful servants of meaning or noisy disrupters of the peace?

13. The Romantic poet, John Keats, claimed that 'we hate poetry that has a palpable design upon us – and if we do not agree seems to put its hand its breeches pock'. Apply his comment to this selection of poems. Do any seem to have a 'palpable design' on the reader? If so, how does the poet want us to respond?

14. Each student should crunch the poem down to one word per line. Discuss this process as a class. Project the poem so the whole class can see it and start the crunching process by indicating and then crossing-out the function words from each line. Now discuss which of the remaining words is most important. This will also give you an opportunity to refer to grammatical terms, such as nouns and verbs. Once each line has been reduced to one word, from this list, pupils should crunch again. This time all that should remain are the five most important words in the whole poem. Now they need to write two or three sentences for each of these words explaining exactly why they are so important and why the poet didn't choose any of the possible synonyms.

'Poetry is only there to frame the silence. There is silence between each verse and silence at the end.'

ALICE OSWALD

Rudyard Kipling, *If*

The white man's burden

Journalist, short story writer and novelist probably best known for *The Jungle Book*, Rudyard Kipling [1865-1936] has been called the 'Bard of Empire' and 'The Prophet of British Imperialism'. Though Kipling's narrative skills and technical virtuosity, especially his dexterity with metre, are almost universally admired, his political views, particularly those concerning race, nationality and Empire are problematic for many modern readers. In short, Kipling idolised the British Empire. And we don't have to be post-colonial critics to take a rather different, more nuanced perspective to the poet's.

Even in his own time, Kipling complained that his most famous poem, *If*, had been 'anthologised to weariness'. Nevertheless, it continues to appear at the top of readers' polls of favourite poems in English and it contains some of the most quoted lines of verse in the language. Kipling's verse was, and remains, popular with a general readership perhaps because it is 'nearly always obviously intelligible at a first reading,' according to W.G. Bebbington, the editor of my vintage copy of the Methuen anthology of Kipling's poetry, first published in 1964. Fair point, but it's harder to agree with W.G. when he goes on to claim that Kipling's 'verse is classless, general, common in the right sense'. Reading the poetry with the benefit of an extra half-century of perspective, it seems clear that though it may feature plucky chaps doing brave things and though it may express sympathy for working class characters such as the British tommy, Kipling's poetry is very much a product of its period and of a distinctly upper-middle class and unashamedly English sensibility.

I wanna be like you

Famously, *If* outlines a detailed description of an ideal man, according to the tastes and values of the late Victorian/ early Edwardian period. Addressed to

the poet's son, the poem's a kind of instruction kit on how to assemble oneself into a hero. All you have to do, the poet advises the boy, is to develop the following list of admirable qualities, and, hey presto, you'll 'be a man, my son'. These masculine virtues include: the ability to remain calm and clear-headed even in an emergency; being able to cope when under severest strain; to retain self-belief despite the doubts of others about your ability; to be modest about yourself and to be patient; to be scrupulously honest and invulnerable to temptations or corruption; to be thoughtful and reflective, but also, very importantly to be a man of action, someone who gets things done; to show fortitude, tenacity and determination whatever the odds and beyond the call of duty; to never accept defeat; to be courageous and daring; to be an everyman figure who is comfortable with ordinary folk and also at ease with royalty; to be sociable and have friends, but also be self-sufficient; to consistently, at all times, to be busily industrious. If you can just manage that, then you'll inherit the world, 'yours is the Earth and everything that's in it'. It's a very small word, 'if', but a huge amount rides on it in this poem. And the poem is, indeed, as W.G. promised, all intelligible pretty much from a first reading. At times, indeed, the language is incredibly simple, direct and straightforward. Take, for example, the last line of the first stanza: 'And yet don't look too good, nor talk too wise'. It's composed entirely of extremely ordinary words, all of them monosyllables, arranged in straightforward syntax and their meaning is literal. But, if Kipling's language is so very ordinary, how comes his poem is so memorable and quotable? The answer lies in three things; his use of antithesis, his mastery of metre and control of rhyme.

The king of the swingers

Many of the poem's lines are constructed thought the arrangement of paired opposites. The superior man, for instance, can 'keep' his head when other people are 'losing theirs'; he can 'trust when others 'doubt'; he can face both 'Triumph and Disaster'' neither 'foes' nor 'friends' can hurt him' he can 'talk to crowds' and also 'walk with Kings' and so forth. The rhythm set up by this two-handed pattern, it's 'this, but not that' doubleness, is underscored by subtle variations in the poem's metre and rhyme scheme. The poem's first line, for example, has eleven syllables and five iambic beats [stressed syllables are in bold]:

'If **you** can **keep** your **head** when **all** about you'

It's a confident, emphatic, regular iambic pentameter. Starting with a weak, unstressed syllable [down-playing the conditional word 'if'] it also finishes with a weak stress. Kipling employs a cross rhyme scheme, so that the first and third lines rhyme with each other, as do the second and the fourth: 'If **you** can

trust your**self** when **all** men **doubt** you'. Again, eleven syllables and a weak stress at the end creates a small dying off or falling away. With an unstressed

syllable ['you'] after the rhyme sound ['out'], this is what's called a feminine rhyme. In contrast, the second and fourth lines finish with stresses on the rhyme words, 'you' and 'too'. This type is called a masculine rhyme. Examine the next four lines and you'll discover the same, alternating rhyme pattern. In fact, check every line in the poem and you'll find that, like well-drilled soldiers, they all follow the same precise, strict pattern, in this case of weak, strong, weak, strong etc. The sorts of strengths Kipling champions are

contrasted with what he considers unmanly weaknesses. This contrast is encoded in the rhyme pattern of the whole poem.

Grammatically speaking, the whole of *If* is one enormous sentence, 32 lines long. All those dependent clauses beginning 'if this' and 'if that' are piled like layers of rock on top of each other and they only reach the summit in the final two lines of the poem. These last lines complete a truly gigantic, weighty sentence. Another aspect of Kipling's technical mastery is that he manages this single sentence without any apparent strain or compositional awkwardness. Look at his poem on the page. You'll immediately notice that it looks solid, four-square, correct and regular. Four substantial, eight line stanzas are arranged in good working order and set going with a metre you could set your watch by and a strict, alternating rhyme scheme. Without exception, all the rhymes are full, well-oiled ones that are slotted precisely into place. No half-rhymes weaken the poem's force or introduce disharmonies. A few of these rhymes are ingenious, such as 'nerve and sinew' with 'nothing in you' and 'unforgiving minute' with 'everything that's in it', but, mostly, they are neat, well-fitted, but not too showy or ostentatious. In other words, Kipling's poem operates like a well-maintained machine and it heeds his own advice by not trying to 'look too good, nor talk too wise'. There are only small variations in the otherwise uniform metre. In the sixth line of the second stanza the poet switches the first metrical foot from an iamb to a trochee. The ear picks this up because all the lines before this have marched to the same iambic beat. The variation gives a little extra sonic push to the verb, 'twisted' and the line itself is suitably just a little bit bent out of shape.

The open-air pulpit

Insightfully, W.G. Bebbington commented that in Kipling's poems 'he and his characters and personifications speak out strongly and in regular rhythm, as though to be heard in the back row'. Certainly, Kipling wished for his poetry to be accessible to non-specialist readers and this helps account for its continuing popularity. And, indeed, Kipling is a poet how speaks out strongly, unambiguously in manly, well-marshalled verse. As befits a poem supposedly addressed to a child, there's not much in *If* that's very taxing on our brains. A hundred years before Kipling, the Romantic poet, John Keats advised readers to distrust poems that have a 'palpable design' on their readers. An extreme case of a tendency in Victorian verse to preach moral lessons at its readers, Kipling's poem is, of course, a sort of morality instruction kit and it reads as if should be declaimed in strident, ringing tones from a lectern or pulpit. Its 'palpable design' is overtly rhetorical, didactic and moralistic. Designed to be inspirational and galvanising, it extols and promotes a specific ideal of manliness. Perhaps a modern audience might be suspicious of this high rhetorical mode, feel a little patronised even and remain unconvinced by the  poet's unswerving confidence in his worldview. Though we must admire the poet's technical virtuosity, it's not easy for us to agree with all his sentiments. For example, Kipling's ideal man is buttoned-up, stiff-lipped, emotionally repressed. Moreover, more troubling, is the Imperial age assertion that the earth and 'all that's in it' must inevitably become his son's, if he can become this capitalised Man. What would happen, for argument's sake, if, by some terribly misfortunate roll of the tricksy dice of fate, you turn out not to be

English, but a foreigner? [Worse still if you happen to be one of what Kipling calls elsewhere the 'sullen peoples']. Or, heaven forefend, what if you're unlucky enough to be born female? If you are the victim of either of these calamities, how do you go

about inheriting the earth by fulfilling your potential? Of is such an entitlement the preserve only of men and upper middle class white ones especially? Is inheriting the Earth solely the white man's burden to take up?

'Crunching' a poem means reducing each line to the single most important word. Obviously, this is a matter of opinion and interesting discussion can be generated through comparing different people's crunches of poems. Here's ours for Kipling's poem.

If crunched:

HEAD - LOSING - TRUST - ALLOWANCE - WANT - LIES - HATRED - WISE - DREAM - THINK - DISASTER - IMPOSTORS - TRUTH - TRAPH - BROKEN - BUILD - HEAP - RISK - AGAIN - BREATHE - FORCE - SERVE - HOLD - WILL - CROWDS - KINGS - HURT - NONE - IF - RUN - EARTH - SON!

Louis MacNeice, *Prayer before Birth*

What's the most unusual narrative perspective you've come across in a novel, short story or poem? Recently the novelist Ian McEwan has re-written the story of *Hamlet* from the perspective of the prince as a foetus in his betraying mother's womb. Clearly this choice of point of view is more of a challenge on the large scale or a novel than it is on the miniature one of a poem. But why choose this perspective, or any unusual or alien perspective in the first place? The point, surely, is to show us something familiar in a new light, from a new angle. According to the influential Russian Formalist critic, the marvellously named, Vicktor Schlovsky the repetitive nature of modern life and modern habits deaden our responsiveness to the world around us. Literature 'defamiliarises' the world to refresh our appreciation and understanding of it. Okay, but why write specifically from the perspective of a foetus?

Well, clearly, we associate babies with innocence and purity. As yet, the poem's narrator has not been touched, or perhaps contaminated, by interaction with the outside world. And because they're pre-birth they express fear and concern about the impact the world might have on that innocence. A foetus is also entirely vulnerable, incapable of defending itself, reliant entirely on the protective instincts it elicits in others. Though, we are all always developing, the younger we are the faster the rate of development, so foetus's are especially impressionable and malleable, their development shaped by their environment in a more profound way than older people are. In MacNeice's poem the foetus will become what the world turns it into.

The black racks

And the world appears a frightening, threatening place in this poem. The opening stanza introduces fear of nasty beasts, both natural and supernatural. These are the fears of a child's imagination, 'blood-sucking bats' and 'club-footed ghouls'. These monsters soon give way to a more disturbing source of fear, humans. Rather than nurture or care or love or protect the new-born baby, the narrator fears the world will imprison, drug, trick and torture it on 'black racks' and 'roll' it in 'blood-baths'. The fears escalate alarmingly as the imagery becomes gruesome. The third stanza provides some respite, with images of a better, kinder, more nurturing world, one that is rooted in nature. But this respite doesn't last long. Soon MacNeice is describing how we have to play different 'parts' like actors in our own lives, how we have to endure lectures and hectoring, put up with being laughed and frowned and cursed at, even by our own children. He also warns of the dangers of men who are bestial or fanatical. And in the fourth stanza the speaker expresses a deep sense of helplessness.

The change of verb in the opening refrain to, 'I am not yet born; forgive me' signals that the violence, damage and sin are inevitable and inescapable. Throughout the fourth stanza the individual's lack of agency is emphasised. The child will become like a puppet, driven and controlled by external forces: 'The sins in me the world shall commit';

'when they murder by means of my hands'. A similar idea is expressed in seventh stanza where the poem's speaker imagines themselves transformed into a killing machine, a 'lethal automaton'. Lacking individuality, stripped of free-will and self-determination, dehumanised as a 'thing' and diminished to just a 'cog' in a 'machine', the speaker becomes a weapon primed for someone else's use. The fact that the forces dragooning, using and controlling the speaker are a faceless, anonymous 'they' and 'those' makes them more sinister. We are not given any sense of who or what these forces are; we only know the individual cannot resist their power and that their power will be abusive.

The poem ends with three similes expressing the speaker's fear that they will become helplessly insignificant: They will be blown around like 'thistledown', so lacking in humanity they will be like a 'stone' and so insubstantial that they could be spilt like 'water'. The unformed malleability of the speaker is underlined by the fact that he/she transforms from a machine, to a cog, to down, to water and to a stone in the space of a few lines. Bleakly, rather than accept this fate, the speaker moves into imperative mode, addressing the reader directly with the short, blunt phrase, 'Otherwise kill me'. After this truncated final line there is nothing but white space.

An engine of hope

The content of the poem might be rather bleak, but it's delivered with an energy that hints at the capacity of the individual to resist and shape their own destiny. To see how the rhythmical aspect of the poem works, we'll take one example, and look at it in some detail. Here's the second stanza with the stressed syllables in bold:

'I **fear** that the **hum**an **race** may with **tall walls wall** me,
with **strong drugs dope** me, with **wise lies lure** me,

on **black racks rack** me, in **blood-baths roll** me'

The metre here is irregular, shifting between the first line and the following two. It starts with a skipping rhythm, generated by a combination of an anapaestic pattern [unstress, unstress, stress] with clearly unstressed words ['that the' and 'may with'] which make the rhythm more pronounced. The end of this line, and the following ones, are more stressy, as five times in a row stressed words are piled up consecutively. The effect is enhanced by MacNeice's use of internal rhymes such as 'tall walls' and 'black racks' and alliteration, such as 'drugs dope' and 'lies lure'. Forming a rapid and repeated DUM-DUM-DUM-dum pattern, these individual stressed monosyllables sound like bullets in a volley of gunfire - 'tall walls wall me'; 'strong drugs dope me'; 'black racks rack me'.

Great energy and rhetorical momentum is generated by the combination of metre, syntax and word choices. And the metrical pattern that runs throughout the poem, albeit with some variations, is MacNeice's invention, an expression of creative freedom and individuality. This muscular counterforce is also embodied in the poem's stanza form. Noticeably the stanzas grow in length, like a new baby and their form is irregular. Two stanzas are tercets and two are quatrains, with others ranging from a couplet to ten lines. And even their growth is irregular, in fits and starts, with the sixth stanza, for example, bucking the general pattern of increasing length. Similarly, though the stanzas grow longer, towards the end the lines actually shorten. Apart from in the first line of each stanza the lineation also follows no pre-set order or regularised pattern. Hence the poem's development is not predictable.

O hear me

It as if the narrator of the poem, the unborn foetus, is pleading with us to intervene and help or even save them from the degradations of the world. The verbs, 'hear', 'console', 'provide' and so forth suggest a parental responsibility in the reader. Neediness may be toughened up by the imperative form, but there is a sense of desperation. This is particularly evident when MacNeice uses apostrophes, such as the repeated 'O hear me'. That naked, single syllable implies pain and need. 'Hear' is repeated as this suggests that normally we don't listen to the weakest, the most vulnerable and the most innocent. Mostly the speaker seeks protection. But in the third stanza a more positive vision is briefly imagined. The innocent, unborn child's needs are presented as simple, natural sustaining things, such as 'water' and 'grass'. Nature also provides company and the child is so in tune with the natural world that the sky 'sings' to it. This is a rural idyll, a natural sanctuary in stark contrast to the oppressive stanzas that surround it. As in Romantic poetry, Nature also is a moral compass, 'a white light' that is internalised as a 'guide' through the world of experience.

References to innocence and experience and to Romantic poetry might bring William Blake, author of *The Tyger*, to mind. Rejecting the doctrine of original sin, Blake and other Romantics, believed children were innocents, closer to God than adults. Often in Blake's poetry, in particular, interaction with society corrupts the innocent. Though in this way MacNeice's poem could be seen to continuing a long established poetic theme, it also directly reflects the world and the period in history in which the poet wrote it. In the middle of the twentieth century the world was divided by violently opposed political ideologies. The Second World War was a war between countries, but it was also a war of political ideologies, Fascism vs. communism and liberal democracy. 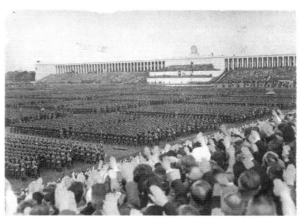 When whole nations and their governments adopt extreme political ideologies that are as potent as any fanatical religion and only the strongest of individuals are able to resist the pull of the group. Others become 'lethal automatons', suppressing their natural human empathy, carrying out orders unthinkingly, like prison guards at concentration camps. The fact that this foetus is aware of the dangers gives it a chance of avoiding these patterns, and instead finding and expressing its own individual self.

Prayer Before Birth crunched:

HEAR - BLOODSUCKING - GHOUL - CONSOLE - WALL - DOPE - LIES - RACK - YET - WATER - BIRDS - GUIDE - FORGIVE - SINS - THEY - TREASON - MURDER - MY - REHEARSE - PARTS - LECTURE - LAUGH - FOLY - DOOM - CURSE - O - GOD - NEAR - FILL - STRENGTH - AUTOMATON - COG - THING - DISSIPATE - THISTLEDOWN - THITHER - WATER - SPILL - STONE - KILL

Written during the Second World War, MacNeice's poem presents a pretty bleak picture of the world the foetus will enter and of the various malign effects it will have. How about writing your own version of the poem? Either you could update it to the world of President Trump, North Korea and crises in our public services, or you could a more positive spin on what the world has in store for the someone born into it today.

Imtiaz Dharker, *Blessing*

A silver rush

Imtiaz Dharker's vibrant poem celebrates the unexpected good fortune of a municipal pipe bursting in a poor neighbourhood of an unnamed city in the developing world and how local people revel in this lucky incident. As the poem's title makes clear, the incident seems like a blessing from a benign God. The excitement of the scene is conveyed by Dharker's choices of visual and sonic imagery. In particular, she describes the released water as being like one of the most valuable precious metals, 'silver'. The poet also chooses a dramatic, dynamic verb, 'crashes' to describe the amount of water spurting from the pipe. 'Crashes' suggests energy, and the sense of sudden speed is enhanced by the use of 'rush' and, more subtly, by a range of sonic devices. For example, liquidy sibilance runs through 'sometimes, the sudden rush'. The mimetic effect is enhanced by a run of assonantal 'u' sounds, while the watery 'sh' of 'rush' echoes in 'crashes'. Lineation further enhances the sense of release: Whereas the first short, stumpy lines of the poem end emphatically with full-stops, the tap of language is turned on after 'the municipal', so that the sentence flows for four lines, over line ends and rhyme sounds, before coming to rest at 'tongues'. Further sonic devices are used to capture the exhilaration of the crowd's reaction; they make an animalistic, loud 'roar'.

Echoing the title, Dharker refers to the crowd in religious terms, describing them as a 'congregation'. The clamour of their desire to get their fair share of the precious silver water shared with them through God's bounty is expressed through a busy, jostling list of words in the last sentence. Again, eagerness, perhaps almost religious fervour is suggested by referring to 'frantic hands'.

Both 'nakedness' and 'children' connote innocence and though the children are 'screaming' this is with joy, not pain. Everything has been transformed for the better by this blessing, so much so that even the sun that had baked the earth into a 'cracked skin' is now a 'liquid sun', as if the water has spread everywhere and cooled everything, even the sun. The glistening transformation wrought by this pipe burst is also expressed by light imagery; the children's 'highlights' are 'polished to perfection' and are 'flashing light' as if they have become angels or small gods. Finally, the universal joy is signalled by the reference to the blessing singing.

Or at least, that's one possible reading of Dharker's poem. Like the poems in Blake's *Songs of Innocence and Experience*, such as *The Tyger*, *Blessing* can be read through an innocent perspective, such as the one above, and be seen as a simple celebration of unexpected good fortune, or it can be read through a less naive, more experienced perspective, a perspective disinclined to find a ramshackle scene of naked children, with small malnourished bones,

desperately competing for water any kind of celebration. <u>If you were to construct a more sober, less positive reading of the poem what evidence would you cite to convince an innocent reader?</u> If you're teaching the poem for the first time with a class, you could ask half the class to construct evidence that the poem is celebratory and the other half to find counter evidence. They could then either debate which reading is right, working in pairs, small groups or as a whole class.

Counterarguments

1. Look at the poem's opening image. This sets the tone and the context for the rest of the episode: 'The skin cracks like a pod'. Clearly, the primary information the image conveys is of such an extreme lack of water that the landscape is parched and the soil broken up into dried patches. But the metaphor of 'skin' adds another dimension. At first we may think that the image could be describing the effect of drought on human skin. This makes the image far more disturbing and emotive.

2. In contrast, the succeeding line is a simple, factual declarative: 'There never is enough water'. Of course water is an essential to all life and the lack of it is potentially fatal. The full stop that concludes this line makes the statement more emphatic and suggests that the situation may be permanent.

3. It is within this water-starved context that the poet invites us to 'imagine the drip' of water as if it is something rare and almost magical. English people don't have to 'imagine' rain. Scarcity of water is implied too by being only a 'drip' that makes only a 'small splash'.

4. While the municipal pipe bursting might appear to be a blessing, this is only a short-term view and only for the people in the immediate vicinity. A more considered perspective would see it as evidence of poorly maintained and/or poorly constructed infrastructure. Other people somewhere else will now not have water because of this accident. If this is a moment of good fortune it is part of a larger context of ill fortune.

5. Nakedness of children is as likely to indicate extreme poverty as it is to connote innocence.

6. While 'screaming' can express excitement and pleasure, the verb also inevitably suggests pain and suffering too. While 'frantic' might suggest eagerness, it also means 'distraught with fear'. They are 'frantic' because they desperately need the water.

7. The description of the blessing singing over the bodies of the children might be celebratory, but it may also bring to mind sacrifices, particularly as the children are described as if they are human remains, just 'small bones'. An ominous, disturbing image is created, not a celebratory one.

8. Finally these bones are 'small'. While this might signal that they are children, it could just as well imply that the children are malnourished.

So, which side of the argument do you find more convincing? To view the bursting of a municipal water pipe as a real blessing would be naive, wouldn't it? To read it the accident this way indicates a superstitious mindset when a more practical one would be of far more benefit to the people in this anonymous city. If this incident is an example of the blessing of some sort of benevolent deity, why doesn't the same deity provide sufficient water in the first place? Why is there 'never enough water'? Surely that's the key point.

Blessing crunched:

SKIN - NEVER - TIN - GOD - RUSH - FORTUNE - SLIEVER - FLOW - ROAR - CONGREGATION - CHILD - BUTTS - BRASS - FRANTIC - NAKED - SCREAMING - PERFECTION - LIGHT - SINGS - BONES

Souvenir of Wembley 1924

INDIA

Sujata Bhatt, *Search for my Tongue*

Speaking the self

What are the fundamental aspects of your identity? Your nationality, your gender, your race? Perhaps your age, the books or music you like, how you dress? Your religion or moral values, the culture you live in, your family? The language you speak in and use? Are these aspects all fixed? Which ones might change over time and why or how might they change?

Sujata Bhatt's poem, *Search for My Tongue*, concerns one of the most important questions facing contemporary multicultural society; how can a person ensure that moving countries, learning new languages or developing new identities does not lead to loss of their original identity? Bhatt's own personal experience has influenced her writing: she has a dual Indian and American identity, and her poem draws on the own ongoing challenges of staying connected to her Indian roots, as she moved to America to study English and feared the fluency of her native tongue diminishing. From the poem's title, Bhatt introduces her extended image of the 'tongue', both the literal organ of communication and also a metaphorical representation of language and identity. Indeed, Bhatt herself said in an interview that 'I have always thought of myself as an Indian who is outside India … That's the deepest layer of my identity'. Bhatt's biographical experience, then, undoubtedly influences the themes of *Search for My Tongue*, particularly the challenges of belonging to multiple cultures.

Bhatt's use of the first person narrative voice draws readers into the experience of reconciling her Indian culture and birth language of Gujarati with her anglicised identity and adoption of a second language, English. Nevertheless, *Search for My Tongue* is not simply a personal exploration of identity. The poem's free verse and comparisons between 'mother tongue' and 'foreign tongue' draw on the universal challenge of reconciling one's native culture and language with a new identity. Bhatt explores more widely the mixed emotions that come with living in a foreign country and the fear of losing touch with one's birth place. This ambivalence also influences the structure of Bhatt's poem. The ongoing enjambment, for instance, suggests the speaker's tumbling, uncontrolled thoughts and anxieties about losing her cultural heritage. One particularly effective example is, 'And if you lived in a place you had to /speak a foreign tongue'. The placement of the verb 'speak' at the start of the line neatly captures Bhatt's belief that it is the challenges of speaking and learning a new language that most threaten her sense of self.

However, the structure of the poem does not solely suggest confusion or a lack of control. There's an underlying confidence and pride that emerges through Bhatt's deliberate division of the poem's one stanza into three sections: English, Gujarati, then English. Despite the speaker's inevitable fear and confusion, she nevertheless recognises the enduring importance of her mother tongue. It is placed at the very heart of the poem's structure, reflecting the centrality of her first language to her identity. The speaker frames the Gujarati with her 'foreign tongue', English, as this is an outer layer of her identity. Even though moving countries and learning new languages will always be tricky, the tripartite phrase and natural imagery describing how her 'mother tongue 'grows longer, grows moist, grows strong veins' demonstrate the speaker's certainty that her Indian identity will always remain integral. Bhatt has made the interesting choice of writing the poem in present tense. This reinforces how relevant the poem's central ideas are to the world today, with the imagery of 'grows' implying that whilst identity is always subject to change when learning new languages and living in new places, one's native tongue will remain always present and 'strong'.

The colonised word

Let's return to the poem's inescapably mixed feelings. It is important to explore the multiple interpretations of *Search for My Tongue*, beyond the fact that it reflects Bhatt's own biographical background and an eventual celebration of one's native culture. In addition to Bhatt's personal sense of lost identity and the structural development from a fear of losing identity to a confidence that the 'mother tongue' will always remain, her poem also has a

possible political purpose, as it touches on colonisation and the British Empire. It could be argued that Bhatt, herself an Asian poet, is criticising the colonisation of India and the imposition of westernised laws and language. Certainly, the two tongues are presented as in competition, even conflict, with each other. For a while the colonising English tongue seems to have the upper hand and its dominance leads to the decay of the indigenous tongue. But the latter survives in the subconscious, in the poet's dreams. In the end, the native tongue returns, captures the intruder, 'ties it 'in knots' and 'pushes' it 'aside'. Switch culture and language for tongue, and literature or the arts for dreams, the poet for India, and a post-colonial reading of the poem becomes apparent. And the poem, appears to carry a message of hope, even of triumph: The colonised culture pushes the coloniser aside to rediscover its own supressed beauty, which grows stronger and 'blossoms'. However, the complexities of the inter-relationship are demonstrated by the fact that this section of the poem is in the coloniser's language, English.

The middle section of the poem had deliberately alienated Western readers [who are unlikely to be fluent in Gujarati]. Most readers must rely on the English translation: this doubling of languages is not only a representation of the speaker's dual identity and reconciliation between her first and second languages, but also a challenge to us to experience the isolation and estrangement faced by migrants when first moving to a new country and having to learn a new language.

The poem's conversational structure also draws out the twin themes, both of feeling secure in one's identity and implicitly critiquing the dangers of colonisation. The emphatically placed pronoun 'You', the first word of the poem, creates an immediate sense of a conversation. Is the addressee the universal reader, who may or may not have direct experience of moving to a new country? Or is this 'you' perhaps a reference to the ignorant 'other', the coloniser? In the line 'if you had two tongues in your mouth' the plural suggests almost physical unpleasantness and a sense of intimate intrusion. The conditional tense 'if' is perhaps a reminder that this is not a universal experience, but one that everyone must understand. Whoever 'you' are, you must be able to understand the experience of a migrant, or any individual fearful of losing their home language and cultural heritage.

Repetition, repetition, repetition

The second person, conversational 'You' is only one example of Bhatt's frequent use of repetition throughout Search for My Tongue. First, there is a sense of Bhatt's own confusion in trying to retain her original culture whilst being part of something new. By repeating the noun 'tongue' in different contexts, as the 'mother tongue', the 'foreign tongue', the 'other tongue', she shows the never-ending challenges of maintaining a sense of self whilst trying to juggle multiple language and adjust to a new country without losing ties with her place of birth. By repeating the 'tongue', too, she can play with the subjective meaning of language and, rather than be controlled by it, gain a sense of empowerment. The 'tongue' can be both her home language and her second language, and it is possible to move countries without forgetting her

50

cultural heritage.

Bhatt also introduces and repeats the metaphor of a plant: 'the bud opens, the
bud opens in my mouth'. This is a
frequent trope in poetry, of course,
with the 'bud' symbolising new life
and hope, but Bhatt places this
natural imagery in a new context, as
a symbol of her own language, which
she now knows will continue to grow.
By associating her first language with flowering, Bhatt implies it is something
both natural and beautiful.

This celebratory imagery towards the end of the poem provides a stark
contrast to Bhatt's earlier use of the plant metaphor, which focused on death
rather than the promise of new life. Again, Bhatt employs repetition to
emphasise her fear of her 'mother tongue' dying, having been usurped by her
new and 'foreign' language and culture. She addresses the second person
speaker to argue that 'your mother tongue would rot,/ rot and die in your
mouth/ until you had to spit it out'. Her conditional tense suggests that the
experience she describes is inevitable. The anaphora of 'rot' creates a harsh,
despondent tone and the image is intimate, tactile and almost disgusting -
imagine having a mouth full of rot... Like a plant, a first language is something
natural and needs ongoing nurturing to survive. There is, too, an interesting
structural repetition here, the first 'in your mouth' mirrored by 'in my mouth'
towards the end of the poem; this echoed phrase, combined with the subtle
change of pronoun, captures her growing self-confidence that her native
language will not be forgotten. It is as if the poet is saying: 'my' culture will not
be lost at the expense of 'your culture'.

A festival of words
Although the first section of *Search for My Tongue* conveys the speaker's
initial distress that her 'mother tongue' and original identity will be forgotten,

the poem's tone changes from fear of the power of the 'foreign' tongue to a mood of celebration. The poet challenges the reader not to see her Gujarati, or any migrant's first language, as something inferior which they should 'spit' out, but rather as something essential and beautiful. As we have noted, Bhatt asserts that her first language 'blossoms' still and will continue to do so – this final positive and present tense verb, extending the plant metaphor even further, illustrates Bhatt's final message; her mother tongue has reasserted itself in her dreams and will, with ongoing nurturing, remain a central part of her identity. And, it is from the enriched mixing of languages and cultures that she will be able to produce her hybrid poetry, finding in this the source of her poetic tongue and distinct bilingual voice.

Search for My Tongue crunched:

MEAN - TONGUE - ASK - YOU - LOST - KNOW - FOREIGN - BOTH - THOUGHT - PLACE - SPEAK - MOTHER - ROT - SPIT - I - DREAM - GROWS - STRONG - KNOTS - BUD - ASIDE- FORGOTTEN - TONGUE-BLOSSOMS

NB
Elsewhere in her poetry, Bhatt more explicitly celebrates the potentially enriching effect of combining languages and cultures and finding deep correspondences and resonances between them. In *Truth is Mute*, for example, she writes beautifully that:

'When she lived on a mountain
among people whose language
she did not know, her own language turned
into a festival of fruits, and a festival of birds.'

52

U.A. Fanthorpe, *Half past two*

Ticking through time

Time. Memory. Childhood. Why do we remember certain events better than others? How accurate is our memory? And what lasting impact can seemingly everyday childhood incidents have on adult perception? In her wry, inventive and gently comic poem *Half Past Two*, Fanthorpe perceives time through the eyes of a child, immediately immersing the reader in a complex exploration of how we struggle to make sense of abstract and subjective concepts. Through the poem's focus on two different attitudes to, and interpretations of, time, a child's and an adult's, we see the impact of early experiences on adult perception, memory [both its truth and unreliability], the power of time and the lasting impact that past moments of interaction and isolation can have on our conscientiousness. Fanthorpe's poem recalls poems by Wordsworth, such as *We are Seven,* which explore the different perceptions of the world children have from adults. There's something too of A.A. Milne here and his poems written in the voices of small children, such as *Now we are Six.*

U.A. Fanthorpe's own life may have influenced the ideas that she focuses on throughout *Half Past Two*. First of all, she did not become a writer until later in her career, after a long stint as a teacher at Cheltenham Ladies' College; the nostalgic tone of this poem [and much of Fanthorpe's other work] may be indicative of her own experience of taking up writing later in life and reflecting on how to make sense of past experiences, rather than describing them in the present moment. By choosing the setting of a school for her poem [and depicting a teacher who does not think through her interaction with the child carefully enough], the poet may be drawing on her own professional understanding of how children think and develop, as well as her own personal interactions with students before leaving the classroom to take up the poetry pen more permanently.

Once upon a time

Half Past Two makes extensive use of the language of fairy tales. This helps to evoke the youthful perspective of the child's observations and his blurred understanding between reality and fiction, particularly when trying to understand a concept, like time, that still lies beyond his comprehension. The poem starts with the stereotypical fairy tale opening, 'Once Upon a SchoolTime'; 'school' may on the surface be an innocent and ordinary setting but, like most fairy tales, it is so often a place with hidden monsters, enemies and challenges to be overcome. Whilst this opening line introduces the poem's emphasis on of childhood naivety, the poem quickly reveals that the boy's memories are shadowed by one particular misunderstanding.

Fanthorpe continues to utilise fairy tale lexis to illustrate how the mysterious half past two detention is to the child. She returns to the deliberately clichéd 'Once Upon' opening later in the poem, but with some subtle changes. Having arrived at his detention, the child 'waited, beyond onceupona,/ Out of reach of all the timefors'; by compounding the opening phrase, 'onceupona', omitting the final 'time', she suggests his increasing confusion. He tries to turn his 'timefors' into something physical that he can 'reach' and recognise: this is a neat reminder to the reader of how we learn when growing up, but also how complex time is to try and make sense of. It is an abstract concept that, once we understand it as adults, we can take for granted, seems straightforward and don't have think about it. For young children, however [and for physicists] it's a more complex and mysterious phenomenon. The 'objectifying' of time, making it something tangible, is something that we continue to do with time in everyday 'adult' conversational language ['I ran out of time', 'I made time to meet you', or 'Time whizzed by during the holidays'].

Through a child's eyes

Although the poem is written from the wryly amused perspective of a third person, omniscient narrator [who makes ironic comments on the narrative, like asides in brackets] it deliberately presents the everyday experience of a

detention through the perspective of a perplexed child and shows how formative tiny moments in childhood can be. The child's simple and structured approach to making sense of the school day is reflected in the  poem's structure of regular, short three line stanzas. Echoed in this tercet form, the language of the poem combines three distinct voices; the child's, their teacher's and the observing narrator's. It is perhaps a deliberate decision by Fanthorpe to include eleven stanzas – one stanza short of the full clock face.

The depiction of the child's perceptions is conveyed by Fanthorpe through diction and non-standard capitalisation. For example, in the solemnly repeated phrase 'Something Very Wrong' we hear the child picking up and repeating his teacher's emphatic words without fully comprehending the nature of his misdemeanour. All he knows is that his teacher has said it was 'something very wrong', so, therefore, it must have been 'something very wrong'. Capitalisation of 'something' reflects how momentous this telling off is in the boy's eyes, whilst the non-specific noun reinforces his lack of real understanding. Moreover, it is also the worst kind of school punishment, one which is administered but not explained, leaving the child feeling guilty for his mistake but with no clear idea of what that mistake actually was and therefore how not to do it again. Worse still, the poor boy fears that he might, in fact, be 'wicked'. The poet suggests the long-term effects that such moments can have, particularly incidents which are not clearly taught and explained; the boy remains ignorant throughout the poem as to the reasons for his scolding. This is emphasised by the parenthesis in the poem's third line, '[I forget what it was]', the brackets an ironic reminder from the first-person narrator that what may have been an offhand comment by the adult teacher could have a lasting impact on the confused child. [The comment also assures us that the misdemeanour wasn't very grave as the narrator cannot even recall what it was.]

Fanthorpe repeats the use of parenthesis, drawing attention to the poem's central themes: how children perceive time differently to adults and how formative childhood memories can be on later perceptions and understanding. The whole third stanza is written as an aside. Again, capitalisation gives the reader insight into the child's thinking, as 'Time', like the upper case 'She' of his teacher, becomes something that he knows is incredibly important, and yet has little understanding of. In fact, the boy does understand time in relation to experiences, but not in any abstract or numerical sense. His innocence and ignorance is contrasted with the teacher's tired thoughtlessness. Emotive adjectives reflect the boy's 'scared' state of mind, with 'wicked' effectively evoking again the language of fairy tales and reminding us how black and white children's thinking can be. If he has done something very wrong, but boy reasons, he must be 'wicked'. Hence the reader sees how tiny moments through an adult's eyes can be huge to a child, suggesting the unseen hurdles faced in the everyday process of growing up.

Growinguptime

Fanthorpe's playful and inventive use of compound words reflects the child's innocence and his attempts to understand the situation. 'Gettinguptime, timeyouwereofftime,/ Timetogohomenowtime, Tvtime' depict the boy's attempts to make sense of the world and his creative approach to breaking down his days. Many of these compounds demonstrate how the child's time is defined by others, particularly parental and school instructions. These examples contrast with the boy's confusion over numerical clock time. This is an alien concept: 'All the important times he knew,/ But not half-past two' because it does not relate in any way to actual experience of the world. The rhyme of 'knew' and 'two' accentuates how little he knows about telling the time and specifically what the mysterious phrase 'half-past two' might mean. Frustratingly for him, he does know that the phrase is of utmost importance. Indeed, the clock itself is defamiliarised by Fanthorpe so that we see as the child does as a face with eyes, but also legs, and a clicking language he cannot decode.

The poem also elevates the status of the child's perceptions; it may not be the necessary or correct way to tell the time, which he will inevitably need to learn for adult life, but the boy's interpretations present his sensible, logical and creative structuring of a mysterious concept, using the information that he does know: He gets up and goes home at the same time, for example, and has fixed 'Grantime', 'teatime' and such markers to make sense of each day. Repetition of the verb 'knew' emphasises the way in which the child [and all of us] builds a picture and explanation of the world through logically connecting things he is sure about to try to understand those things he is unsure of. The verb is a reminder to the reader of how much knowledge we can take for granted in adult life.

Escape to the clockless land

What is it the child ends up remembering most vividly about this experience? Is it the trauma of being told he has done 'Something Very Wrong' and the reflection that he might therefore be 'wicked'? Or is it the worry of waiting for his teacher and not knowing what she meant by 'half past two'? Or is it the confused message the teacher gives him, telling him  when she finally arrives that she has forgotten about his terrible crime and that he should 'run along', as if doing 'Something Very Wrong' really wasn't very important after all? No, it's not any of those things. It's the sense of escaping time that stays with him. The immersion into pure, unreflective sensory experience - the smell of the flowers, the paradoxical noise of silence; immersion into a mystical, spiritual, visionary of oneness with nature and lightness of being when his conscientious seems to float free on an ocean of timelessness. Is this a vision of heaven? Or perhaps a vision of death? Perhaps it is both. But it is certainly a vision of freedom of which all adults whose lives are regulated by clocks can only wistfully dream.

Time to end

Although the first-person interjection, '[I forget what it was]' does imply that childhood traumas are, objectively, less memorable and significant than those faced in adulthood, Fanthorpe captures the complex psychology of a child and, through the deliberately simplistic language and narrative style, reminds readers to occasionally put themselves in a child's shoes and remember how different a small child's perspective is to an adult's more experienced one. Romantic poets, such as William Blake and William Wordsworth, believed that children were the embodiment of innocence, and therefore gave them an elevated, special status. Fanthorpe's poem may perhaps be a critique of how far the haste and stress of everyday life often leads to less time for making proper time to understand the way children think and grow up and explain more challenging concepts in a slower, more thoughtful way.

Half Past Two can also be interpreted as a positive, nostalgic reflection on childhood. The fairy tale lexis, the compound words, the focus on getting told off rather than getting to grips with time's meaning, all portray the contrasting priorities faced in the early years of life compared to the increasing challenges of adulthood. It can therefore also be seen as a celebratory encouragement to enjoy every childhood moment. For both children and adults, Fanthorpe ultimately suggests, time remains beyond our control. We will, like the omniscient narrator, continue to grow older, unable to stay fixed in childhood as the clock continues to tick. For both children and adults, time is subjective, complex and ultimately inescapable.

Half Past Two crunched:

SCHOOLTIME –WRONG –FORGET –SHE – SOMETHING – STAY – CROSS – TIME –SCARED – KNEW – TIME – TIME –TIME –IMPORTANT – HALF-PAST – EYES – TWO – LANGUAGE – WAITED –OUT –ESCAPED – INTO – SILENT – OUTSIDE –MY –SCUTTLING –RUN –SLOTTED – HOME – NEXTTIME –NEVER – CLOCKLESS – HIDES

D.H. Lawrence, *Piano*

Appassionato

Although he was an accomplished and influential poet, D.H. Lawrence [1885-1930] is probably most famous for his controversial novels, such as *Sons and Lovers, Women in Love* and, in particular, *Lady Chatterley's Lover.* Born into a working-class mining family in Nottinghamshire in the late Victorian period, Lawrence was a prodigious and distinctly original artist who also wrote essays, short stories and plays. He remains a highly controversial figure because in addition to expressing radically right wing political views, in his novels Lawrence explored sexuality in a frank manner that was deeply shocking to his contemporaries. Famously when *Lady Chatterley's Lover* was finally published in England in 1960, thirty years after Lawrence's death, its publishers, Penguin, were prosecuted under the Obscene Publications Act. Notoriously Lawrence's novel depicts a passionate sexual relationship between an upper-class lady and her working-class gardener. Despite the controversy, the literary qualities of the novel led to an acquittal that changed the nature of what could be published in England.

Give me five

Recently the poet and academic Simon Armitage has recommended a strategy for reading a poem that avoids the pitfalls of technique spotting.

Armitage suggests that readers pick out around five words or so from a poem and then explore meticulously why the poet may have chosen these specific words rather than synonyms that may have served nearly as well. So, let's try applying the Armitage method to Lawrence's *Piano*, but with a slight variation.

As well as individual words, we're going to choose a phrase or two. Which five words or phrases jump out from the rest of the poem and demand our attention? Pick these for yourself before reading any further. And don't be tempted into peaking at our selection before you've made your own. That'd be cheating. Go on, get the poem right now and pick out your best five words. Don't you dare read ahead until you've done this. We're watching you...

For us, the following words stand out: 'boom'; 'insidious mastery', 'betrays', 'glamour', 'manhood' and 'weep'. We know, we know, that's six. We cheated, just a little. The explosive, onomatopoeic first word in the list, 'boom' seems out of place in a poem describing a woman singing accompanied by a pianist. In the first word of the first quatrain Lawrence had established that the music is playing 'softly' and immediately after 'boom' refers to 'tingling strings'. With its internal rhyme and 'i' sound, sonically that phrase is much lighter than the deeper 'boom'. So, is this just a not very good description perhaps? Maybe, but perhaps 'boom' conveys something of the profound effect of the experience on the poet - it sets off an explosion in his head. Moreover, the sonic tension here echoes a wider tension in the poem in terms of the ambivalent way in which Lawrence presents this experience and, indeed, himself as a character.

Insidious mastery

The second phrase we've selected, for instance, suggests that the experience had a powerful effect, 'mastery', but also an unwelcome one. Normally something 'insidious' has a harmful effect. Moreover, carried over from its Middle French origins the adjective suggests deceit, cunning, treachery and even entrapment. If the memory of a piano playing were a pleasant one, taking Lawrence back to fond childhood memories, why does he use such a negatively charged word? Initially the poet could maintain some emotional distance from the memory the music prompts. He says that he 'sees' 'a child' sitting under the piano. While this is clearly himself, Lawrence remains an observer; he could, for instance, have written 'I am a child again sitting under the piano'. However, by the second stanza this distance between the observer and the observed, the adult poet and his childhood self, has collapsed. The third person 'a child' has transformed into 'me', and furthermore into the 'very heart of me'.

Why does Lawrence resist the tug of the music and the memories it triggers? Why is the effect 'insidious'? It is 'in spite' of himself that the song 'betrays him'. Like 'insidious', 'betray' seems an incongruous and disproportionate word in this context, and like 'insidious' it implies treachery, back-stabbing, harm done. So, it seems Lawrence feels mastered and overwhelmed by the power of song which unlocks memories and releases a surge of strong emotions. Neither his reason nor his will are strong enough to hold back the tide or 'flood' of feelings. And these feelings are so potent because they are of loss and displacement, specifically the loss of a secure, familiar home, the loss of a stable centre of being. This is why the experience is 'insidious' and feels like a betrayal.

Winter inside

Home offered protection; a metaphorical 'winter' was kept 'outside'. It provided comfort too - it was 'cosy'. Moreover, it set a clear sense of direction, purpose and perhaps morality - the 'tinkling piano' was his 'guide'. Notice too the plural pronoun in contrast to the lonely 'I' of earlier in the poem. In photography, a negative is the black and white image from which colour prints used to be produced. Bright objects in real life appear dark on a negative and vice  versa. Reverse the positive details of the home and we get the negative image of what Lawrence wants, but longer has in his life. So, we understand that now, as an adult, the poet feels rootless, unsupported, exposed to the coldness and harshness of a metaphorical winter, desperate, lost and alone. And to add to his woe, he is aware that the bright, warm image of home is in the past, it has gone from him forever and cannot be recovered. And these negatives feelings sweep over him via the music. No wonder then that he resisted their effect.

It might seem odd that Lawrence describes childhood as having a 'glamour'. Possibly rather than the modern associations with celebrity lifestyles, by 'glamour' he means brightness and attractiveness. Perhaps too Lawrence is drawing on older meanings of the word of 'enchantment' and 'magic' which fit with the sense that he has become entranced by the music, memory and emotion. If 'glamour' signals a positive dimension to the experience, his negative feelings are evident in the fact that he describes his susceptibility as emasculating and infantilising. He felt 'mastered' and his 'manhood' is, he says, 'cast down' when he caves into, feels defeated by raw emotion. Clearly, then the poet's feelings are ambivalent.

What impression do you form of Lawrence's character from this poem? He wants to convey a tough manliness that can resist the annoyingly noisy 'clamour' for his attention of the 'great black piano', despite it being played 'appassionato'. Despite his strength, he is, however, mastered. Such is the power of music, of memory and of emotion. Hence while  protesting that he has been betrayed by his feelings the poet simultaneously demonstrates a sensitive, emotional artistic self. Tough and sensitive at the same time. Perhaps this self-conscious self-projection helps explain the inconsistent identification of the poem's speaker with his childhood self. A little distance creeps back into the perspective in the concluding image, for example: 'I weep like a child for the past'. It may also help to explain the mastery Lawrence establishes over the material. While the poem has a lot of enjambment, which suggests the language is flowing free from constraint, like the flood of emotion, this is boxed in and contained by neat, orderly quatrains. And these orderly quatrains each end reassuring with emphatic full stops. If there is a flood, the flood defences appear able to cope. So, for a poem about emotion flooding and overwhelming the manly defences of reason and will, it's a remarkably composed, controlled affair. Tough, manly but also sensitive too.

Piano crunched:

SINGING – SEE – CHILD – MOTHER – INSIDIOUS – BETRAYS – HOME – GUIDE – VAIN – GLAMOUR – MANHOOD - WEEP

Vernon Scannell, *Hide and Seek*

The game of life

What might a simple children's game reveal about the deeper meanings of life? What is life all about, anyway? What achievements do we most value and what obstacles can life throw in our way?

On the surface, Vernon Scannell's poem is a detailed description of one boy's attempts to win a game of hide and seek, before realising that his friends have given up trying to find him and have headed home. Of course, this simple seeming narrative is used to explore more complex and varied ideas. The popular children's game becomes an extended metaphor for the experience of life itself and Scannell focuses, in particular, on the themes of isolation, overcoming obstacles and grabbing the opportunities that come our way. By giving the poem the seemingly simple title *Hide and Seek*, Scannell immediately introduces its multiple meanings: the name of the childhood game at the centre of the poem's plot, but also it can also be interpreted as the obstacles or difficulties in life we may want to 'hide' from, as well as the opportunities and achievements that we 'seek'.

Written from the perspective of the hiding child, the poem employs the unusual perspective of second person. It could be argued, firstly, that the poem is written from the perspective of an external speaker who is addressing the boy, an omniscient voice that guides the boy's decisions and helps him to reflect on his feelings. Or perhaps – and this is perhaps the more intriguing interpretation – a conflict is implied between the boy's internal and external thoughts. The poem's imagery, certainly, reflects his ongoing conflicting emotions: for instance, Scannell juxtaposes light and dark, excitement and fear, noise and silence to show life's ups and downs as well as the boy's mixed feelings. Moreover, these continued contrasts reflect not only the child's fluctuating emotions [after all, he both technically wins the game of hide and seek yet also loses out, leaving it too late to reveal his hiding place] but also the nature of life itself. Like a game of hide and seek, life is full of both pleasure and pain, achievements and challenges, and tough decisions that may often have to be faced alone.

Winners and losers

From the opening lines of the poem, the poet makes clear that the boy is focused on winning this game of hide and seek: 'Call out. Call loud: 'I'm ready! Come and find me!'/ The sacks in the tool-shed smell like the seaside./ They'll never find you in this salty dark'. This is presented as an internal dialogue that the boy is having with himself, the repeated imperative 'Call' at the start of the poem expressing his initial excitement and ambition to win. The immediate use of caesuras conveys fast-moving thoughts, but perhaps also the boy's isolation; there is, after all, no response to his self-instruction. Caesuras also break the flow of the metre, like rhythmic bumps along the road of life itself. Nevertheless, the positive, playful tone soon returns, as the child stays certain that the other children will 'never find' him and he can be crowned the 'hide and seek' champion. The whispering sibilance, of 'sacks', 'shed', 'smell', 'seaside' and 'salty', helps maintain the boy's excited, optimistic tone and echoes the sound of the sea; the boy initially associates his hiding place with the beach setting, stereotypically a place of holidays and happiness.

Scannell captures the competitive spirit of childhood. Remaining concentrated on his ultimate goal of winning throughout the poem when the boy has not been found, he tells himself, 'Out of the shed and call to them: 'I've won!/ Here I am! Come and own up I've caught you!'. Again, the dialogue and repeated simple sentences, combined with repeated exclamation marks, indicate his childlike delight in making sure his success is recognised. On a deeper level, Scannell explores here the ongoing challenges in life; we are forced to compete with others and overcome hurdles in order to achieve. The synaesthetic 'salty dark' in the third line contrasts to the brightness of the 'seaside' and introduces repeated references to darkness, a metaphorical reflection of the boy's own more pessimistic emotions and the inescapability of the more difficult times in life.

The icy face of isolation

Scannell's descriptions of both the boy hiding in the shed and his later realisation that he has been abandoned by his friends are laced with loneliness. The poem's simple vocabulary captures the boy's shifting feelings and the inevitable obstacles he continues to face. The bluntly factual 'The floor is cold' is, on the surface, a simple account of the slightly uncomfortable tool shed surroundings. However, the emotive adjective 'cold'  has greater symbolic significance, reflecting the 'cold' treatment of the boy by the other children and thus reminding the reader of the challenging people and places that adult life will continue to throw in our direction.

The less pleasant imagery increases as the poem continues, as a harsher, monosyllabic style develops. The discomforts of the boy's hiding place become more and more apparent. Again, the second person narrative heightens the poem's emotional intensity, as either the omniscient poet or the boy's internal thoughts remind him that 'Your legs are stiff, the cold bites through your coat;/ The dark damp smell of sand moves in your throat'. The sensual seaside imagery morphs into something uncomfortably intimate and tactile. Again, the confused mixing of senses, synaesthesia, is used, but now the effect is disturbing as the 'dark' 'smell' solidifies to a taste that 'moves' inside the boy's mouth. The alliterative 'dark damp smell' conveys the boy's anxiety and dislike of his surroundings. Scannell's repetition of 'dark' also brings into play the ominous associations of that word - darknesses in all its different shapes and forms. The cold bites here, drawing on the same adjective used earlier to describe the floor, yet with the added intensity of personification, reflecting the boy's increasing fear and awareness of his isolation.

This is not, however, the end of the darkness. Pathetic fallacy is used at the end of the poem: 'The darkening garden watches. Nothing stirs./ The bushes hold their breath; the sun is gone.' Combining the end of the game with the boy's realisation that 'the sun is gone', the poet implies how empty the boy's success is, despite his earlier determination to win at all costs. Having left it too long to reveal his hiding place, he now must celebrate his victory alone. Why do the bushes hold their 'breath'? What are they waiting for or expecting? As well as suggesting the superior power of the surroundings over the boy himself, personification adds to the rising tension. This returns us to the central metaphor of *Hide and Seek*, that this seemingly harmless childhood game represents the bumpy journey of life itself; as in later life, many challenges are beyond our control.

Hiding in blindness

Throughout the poem, Scannell weaves in ominous imagery to remind the reader that this is more than simply a childhood game. As the boy waits in silence to be discovered, he reminds himself that 'You mustn't sneeze when they come prowling in'. The modal verb 'mustn't' reflects how significant this moment is to the boy and the weight he places on his self-instructions. At the start, nothing matters more to him than staying hidden, a reflection not only of his distorted perspective of what it important [a neat reminder of how our priorities develop between childhood and adulthood] but also of the boy's fear. Indeed, this is enhanced by the threatening, animalistic verb 'prowling', turning his competitors into predators. There is a staccato rhythm to the boy's thoughts, structurally embodied here through end stopping, a technique that Scannell repeats on numerous occasions throughout *Hide and Seek*. By fragmenting the poem's flow in this way, the poet captures the boy's disjointed thoughts and fluctuating emotions, as well as his tense uncertainty.

Arguably, the disappearance of the other children marks a turning point in the poem. This is the moment when the boy perhaps should have revealed his location, yet he hangs on just a little too long. The boy believes that they will search elsewhere and then return, convincing himself 'They must be thinking that you're very clever'. Again, caesuras add to the drama of the moment. Scannell hints at the fact that this is not a smooth move by the boy: Assonance in 'Hide in your blindness' emphasises his lack of foresight, that hiding too long would have negative consequences. The repeated  language of negation, too, through the simple imperative 'Don't' reflects how the boy has taken this competition too far.

Where are they?

Scannell concludes the poem with a deliberately ambiguous tone. The bittersweet nature of the boy's victory through the poem's final rhetorical question, 'Yes, here you are. But where are they who sought you?' The conversational tone and unanswered question here can be read in diverse ways. Ostensibly, the ending reflects the boy's simple realisation that they have abandoned the game of hide and seek, moving on elsewhere without letting him know. On a deeper level, this symbolises the poem's central theme of isolation, the impersonal pronouns 'they' and 'you' reinforce the universality of human experience, and the challenging events that everyone inevitably must face.

Before the sun goes down

Sometimes all of us crave and need privacy. At other times, we seek the company of others. Getting this balance can be right is difficult. Spend too long on our own we can grow lonely, self-obsessed, stuck in our ways. Spend too long in society and the inner, contemplative and creative self slips away. Living mostly in their heads and their imaginations, writers, in particular, need some separation, even isolation, from other people and the mundane business of life in order to write. Many writers, for example, have a special room or shed or space separate from the rest of the house, somewhere they can blank out external reality and fully concentrate on their work. But they also need material for their writing, which comes at least in part from interaction with the outside world. And the outside world is also important in another way. Few writers write only for themselves. Most need publishers, reviewers, a readership, money, acclaim. Isolate yourself for too long as a writer, working on your magnificent work, and the public might just forget about you. Little point emerging, blinking, from your creative sanctuary with your triumphant masterpiece clasped in your hand, only to find nobody there, everything silent and the sun already long gone down on your career.

As ever, it is worth considering the extent to which the poet's own experiences may have influenced the themes of his work. Scannell himself left school at 14 to work in a local office – something that was not uncommon at the time. During the Second World War, Scannell enlisted in the army. But after the end of the war in Europe, disgusted by some of the horror he witnessed, he deserted and went on the run. Caught and arrested, Scannell was sentenced

70

to two years imprisonment and spent six months 'one of the harshest penal institutions in Alexandria'[2]. After his release, Scannell had to re-join the army, but deserted again, going into hiding and spending a further two years on the run from the authorities. Hide and seek indeed.

Hide and Seek crunch:

FIND – SEASIDE – YOU – CAREFUL – RISK – COLD – HAPPENS – PROWLING – WHISPERING – HUSHED – BLINDNESS – STUMBLES – GONE – DON'T – BACK – CLEVER – PUZZLED – LONG – BITES – DARK – TIME – UNCURL – WON – CAUGHT – DARKENING – GONE – YOU

NB

Look at the poem on the page. What does this single block of text look like? A rather solid letter 'I' perhaps? One way of foregrounding the effect of this structural device would be to present the poem the first time to a class in a different form. Re-arrange it, for example, as prose or in couplets or quatrains or irregular sized stanzas. If you choose the prose option, ask them to re-arrange this as a poem. If you choose the various stanza options get them to conjecture about the significant of these, before revealing Scannell's starkly, singular, unbroken form.

[2] https://en.wikipedia.org/wiki/Vernon_Scannell

William Shakespeare, *Sonnet 116*

Type this sonnet into the great modern oracle named google and the following information is revealed:

Sonnet 116 is about love in its most ideal form. The poet praises the glories of lovers who have come to each other freely, and enter into a relationship based on trust and understanding. The first four lines reveal the poet's pleasure in love that is constant and strong, and will not 'alter when it alteration finds'.

Number one

Hence perhaps the popularity of this sonnet at weddings. In the pantheon of famous love poems, sonnet 116 most be close to number one. And with good reason.Firstly it's a sonnet, obviously, a form intimately linked with love. Its opening line declares true love as a platonic, intellectual ideal, 'a marriage of true minds'. It is a marriage because it is shared between two people - it is mutual, not lopsided or unbalanced. Love is also constant, true, never altering or warping or deforming into something else. Love is, of course, an abstract noun, but in Shakespeare's formulation it is so strong that it becomes almost a material object. And its physicality is robust, solid, stable, substantial; a source of strength it cannot be bent or shaken even by enormous pressure.

Even when its rejected, true love remains steadfast, it does not 'remove' itself. However rough life may get, whatever metaphorical 'tempests' we may face, love is definite and dependable -an 'ever-fixed mark' we can navigate with certainty by. Further metaphors for life's vicissitudes configure the individual as an imperilled boat ['wandering bark'] at sea, vulnerable to tides and bad weather.Love is a source of beauty and light, above us, a 'star' that guides us home, a little like the lighthouse in our illustration, only far better. In both of these cartographical images love gives us a sense of orientation, direction and security.

Conventionally sonnets follow a question/ answer, or call/ response form, with a hinge line falling between the opening octave and closing sestet. This hinge, or volta, signals the turn in the argument. Sonnet 116 rolls on after the octave without any turn, building a sense of onward momentum in one direction.Love, we learn, is not the plaything or servant of a capitalised Time. Physical beauty may be swept away by Time's grim reaper-like 'bending sickle' but love continues beyond the loss of good looks, 'even' to life's very end. And love is courageous, continuing constantly, loyally, selflessly 'even' to the rather onimously Mordor-sounding 'edge of doom'.

And, if you weren't convinced enough by that twelve line barrage of imagery, Shakespeare puts his reputation as a writer on the line. If he hasn't got this exactly right, then he never wrote a true word and, moreover, nobody in the history of the entire world has actually really been in love. Reverse engineer the statement: people have fallen in love, Shakespeare most certainly did write rather a lot, as the current example we're reading neatly illustrates, QED his definition of the nature of true love must be correct.

We can trust Shakespeare because he is at such pains to distinguish true love from something very close to it, something that might readily pass for love to a less astute and forensic observer. And he's also been puzzling over the nature of love during the previous 115 sonnets. The fact that true love and a counterfeit version, or some lesser emotion such as lust or infatuation, are hard to tell apart is emphasised by Shakespeare's word choices. Particularly significant are the sequence of paired words in the opening lines:

- Love / not love
- Alters / alteration
- Remover / remove

Such oppositions, of course, are food and drink to structuralist readers. For us the question is why didn't Shakespeare choose synonyms, such as 'changes' or 'leaver'? The point, surely is the words are so similar to emphasise the fact that 'love' and its counterfeit, 'not love', are also very similar and hard to distinguish from each other. Just as each of these paired words share most of the same letters, so true and counterfeit love share many of the same features. Small, seemingly insignificant, changes to the words, such as adding just one extra letter, an 'r' to the end of 'remove', utterly changes the grammatical function of

these words; so, minute differences differentiate true from counterfeit love. And these small variations lead to radical different, opposite actions. Such small differences, in other words, have enormous implications.

Let me/ let me not

So goes the case for reading *Sonnet 116* innocently as perhaps the ultimate attempt to define and celebrate true love in poetry. But there's another, more troubling reading that runs against this dominant interpretation. To start we might consider to whom the poem is addressed. In total Shakespeare wrote 154 sonnets in this sequence and he addresses a number of characters in the poems, including a handsome young nobleman who seems to be his patron, a 'dark lady' with whom he is also in love,as well as various rivals and enemies, both corporeal [another poet and admirer] and abstract [time, fancy, selfishness etc]. Scholars are not certain about the identity of these characters, though Henry Wriothesley, the dashing 3rd Earl of Southampton and Shakespeare's patron, pictured on the previous page, is the frontrunner as the young man. He certainly looks pretty sultry. In many of the sonnets Shakespeare worries about his own love being rejected by either or both the young man and the dark lady, who also seem to have a dalliance with each other - a classic love triangle. In sonnet 91, for example, after cataloguing all the young man's most excellent virtues Shakespeare concludes that he is 'wretched in this alone, that thou mayst take / All this away and me most wretched make'. Perhaps not his finest couplet, but the fear of rejection's palpable.

Scholarship tells us that the first 120 or so of the sonnets are addressed to the young nobleman and the last 25 or so to the 'dark lady'. <u>Doesn't the opening phrase 'let me not' suggest Shakespeare would actually rather like to 'admit' or introduce obstacles or impediments?</u>Perhaps the 'marriage of true minds' is not between Shakespeare and the poem's addressee; after all Shakespeare could not marry the Earl of Southampton. If that is the case then Shakespeare himself, as the rejected lover, might be seen as the impediment to the 'marriage'. This radically reverses the way we read the next lines. In fact their tone could now be read as accusatory, not celebratory.

In this reading, Shakespeare is distinguishing his true constant, unchanging love with the more fickle love of a lover who has altered and spurned him. The addressee, let's call him Henry, has removed and is wandering [to a different lover, perhaps the 'dark lady'] but Shakespeare heroically and selflessly and unrequitedly loves him still. And will not do anything now to get in the way of their relationship, he promises. Perhaps this explains that sudden exclamatory, emotional 'o, no!' Read in this way, all the celebratory and celebrated metaphors of love become coded and barbed, implying that Henry has fallen for a lesser, essentially counterfeit love. For example, the 'rosy lips and cheeks' do sound rather female as well as youthful, so Shakespeare would be insinuating that the love that has attracted Henry is superficial compared to his own timeless love. It also helps explain the otherwise overly ominous note sounded by the 'edge of doom'.

Shakespeare contemplating the 'edge of doom'/ a
reader contemplating a 'leap' of interpretation

If, jilted, Shakespeare will have to love on from afar, removed from his beloved, this will feel like undertaking a journey to Mordor. Perhaps too, this subtextual, against the grain reading, might account for the oddly off notes generated by the sonnet's imperfect rhyming. Even accounting for changes in pronounciation over time, 'love / remove', 'come / doom' and 'proved/ love' seem unlikely to have ever harmonised fully.

Read this way, the poem is the equivalent of smiling through gritted teeth. Or a fist of steel in a velvet glove. Superficially it seems to be celebrating a couple's relationship, but really it is making pointed comments. And, if we accept this, the poem itself becomes ironic: Shakespeare professes to not wanting to put any barriers up between the lovers; then he writes a poem that itself is a potent intervention and weighty impediment.

Convinced? Disagree? We'd have to read that opening line about 'true minds' as being pointed or sarcastic. Perhaps we're in danger of bending the lines to suit our interpretation. And aren't we making a huge assumption that the speaker in the poem is acutally Shakespeare and that the content is autobiographical? That seems to be a rather dangerous assumption for a poet more famous as a playwright. That said, even if we shed the autobiographical reading, the poem could still be addressed to a beloved by a character whose lover has been rejected. You'll have to decide. Or, as in the examination you'll be asked to argue for and against a critical proposition about one of these poems, perhaps you don't need to take a leap one way or another.

Maybe the opening of sonnet 117 might give us a clue: 'Accuse me thus: that I have scanted all/ Wherein I should your great deserts repay'. Hardly sounds like a joyous continuation of a celebration of true love, does it? But, then again, scholars argue over the correct sequence of the poems and, indeed, whether they even form a coherent sequence.

Let me not crunch

TRUE – IMPEDIMENTS – ALTERS – REMOVER – EVER-FIXED – NEVER – STAR – UNKNOWN – FOOL – SICKLE – LOVE – DOOM – ERROR – NEVER

John Keats, *La Belle Dame sans Merci*

A man in love

Scholars seem to agree that the Romantic poet, John Keats, had a rather problematic attitude towards women. Though he was attracted to young women, he was also repelled by what he considered to be their flirtatious and untrustworthy behaviour. In particular, the poet had a long, difficult relationship with his beloved, Fanny Brawne. Keats's letters show that he often worried about whether Fanny Brawne really loved him and that he was jealous of any attention she received from other men. Simultaneously he fretted about being trapped in their relationship:

'Ask yourself my love whether you are not very cruel to have so entrammelled me, so destroyed my freedom'.

And love itself, he sometimes described in his letters as an affliction: 'A man in love I do think cuts the sorryest figure in the world'.

Though, as we will see, this poem can be read in many ways, and although not all its mysteries can be neatly resolved, at its simplest level, dressed in medieval garb, supernaturalied and mythologised, featuring a character entrammelled and imprisoned, *La Belle Dame Sans Merci* expresses Keats's ambivalent feelings about the power of love, sex and women.

A few years before completing *La Belle Dame* Keats had written in *Edymonion* that 'A thing of beauty is a joy forever', one that will 'keep a bower quiet for us, and a sleep / full of sweet dreams'. His *Ode to a Grecian Urn* concludes with the resounding declaration that 'beauty is truth, truth beauty' and Keats's poetry, as a whole, can be seen as a quest after beauty. But *La Belle Dame Sans Merci* upsets his equation of beauty with truth: Certainly, the titular character is beautiful, but the knight is mistaken when he thinks she loves him 'true'. Rather than bringing him peace, the knight is left the sorriest figure, 'haggard and woebegone', 'alone and palely loitering'. Beauty in this poem is entrancing, captivating. But it is also deceptive, dangerous, draining. Perhaps this is why, simultaneously some sort of goddess and demon, the figure of La Belle Dame cast such a powerful spell on Keats's imagination.

A safe distance?

Keats's ballad features two narrators - a frame narrator who begins the poem and asks questions, and a knight who takes up the narration in the fourth stanza. Mysteriously the frame narrator disappears from the scene, diminishing to only a faint linguistic echo in the last stanza, leaving a lingering sense of incompleteness to the poem. This begs the question, <u>what is the function of the frame narrator and why does he, or she, vanish</u>? Firstly, the narrator twice asks questions of the knight; what is wrong with him and why he is wandering about like a lost soul. Use of the apostrophe, 'O', implies concern for the knight, indicating that the narrator is not merely an objective or disinterested observer - somehow they are emotionally involved in the poem's events. As well as setting the scene and witnessing the knight's anguished state, the narrator also seeks an explanation for the pale knight's strange, wandering behaviour.

The literal minded among us may wonder what exactly the narrator was doing near this silent, withered lake, where he [or she] happens upon the 'haggard' knight. Perhaps Keats is suggesting that the narrator is potentially another victim of La Belle Dame Sans Merci, somebody who has also strayed from the safety of civilisation and from the masculine sphere of action. Just as the knight is warned by the dead men, so the knight warns the narrator. The narrator seeks answers from the knight perhaps so that [s]he can avoid meeting the same fate. If we accept this reading, Keats uses the narrator to amplify the story, to suggest that there is something universal in the pattern of seduced and betrayed men. Unwarned, the narrator might have followed the knight who has, in his turn, followed the 'pale warriors' to the elfin grot. Initially it is as if the narrator is asking us their questions, which places us, albeit momentarily, in the position of the knight. Hence the poem implies the reader too can be drawn into its seductive narrative.

There is another way of looking at this. As we've said, on one level Keats's poem is about the dangers of falling in love with a beautiful, but untrustworthy woman and dramatises his fear that women may betray men. At the heart of the poem there appears a pretty straightforward story of a short-lived love affair followed by a break-up. However, Keats wishes to explore and understand his feelings by getting some perspective on them, examining them from a distance. Hence he supernaturalises and medievalises the story, transforming it into a timeless myth. The use of the two narrators reflects the way in which the poet tries to distance himself from his experience, adopting the seemingly safe position of frame narrator as well as of the armoured and armed figure of a knight. The fact that he slips so seamlessly from outside observer to protagonist suggests the power of the story to dissolve such defensive strategies, to draw Keats in. Similarly, the knight's armour offers him no protection against the bewitching Belle Dame.

The knight

The transition from narrator to character could have been indicated using speech marks. Keats employs these to indicate the speech of the woman and the dead men too. <u>So why not use them when the knight speaks?</u> If the poet had wanted to distinguish clearly between the two speakers he could also have given them different language, in terms of register, vocabulary and rhythms. Taken together, it seems that Keats wished to deliberately blur any distinction between the two characters. They are either two potential victims, or essentially two versions of the

same person, one before and the other after encountering La Belle Dame.

Obviously the knight fits with the Romantic medieval atmosphere of the poem. The medieval setting also implies that this is an archetypal story, a timeless pattern of behaviour repeated eternally. This would all be true if the character were a wandering minstrel, or such like. A 'knight', however, has connotations of an ideal man: nobility of character, masculine strength and power, action, heroism, the highest standards of chivalry etc. In medieval Romances knights fight and vanquish monsters to win the hand of beautiful, virtuous maidens. In Keats's twist of the story, the beautiful, virtuous maiden turns out to be the monster. And if a knight and other noble characters, such as kings and princes, can be so easily undone what chance for ordinary mortals? Or, indeed, for poets?

The effect La Belle Dame has on the knight is specific:

1. He loses blood and looks ill; he is exhausted, enfeebled and feels 'forlorn': 'O what can ail thee'... 'fever'... 'palely'... 'haggard'... 'woebegone'.
2. He is isolated ['alone'] and stripped of his active, heroic role - he is away

from battle, aimlessly 'loitering'. He has become the wandering ghost of his former self. Once a man of noble action, all he can do now is to pass on his dreadful warning.

3. Moreover, his appearance suggests that the knight has been emasculated. Both similes in the third stanza use flowers associated with feminine beauty, the lily and the rose. The process of his loss of male power can be traced through the verbs used in the middle section of the poem. On first meeting La Belle Dame, the knight appears to be in control. He is the active subject of the verbs 'I met', 'I made', 'I set'. These three little, simple monosyllabic verbs, coming at the start of three successive stanzas, summarise a swift, bold courtship. The gallant knight sweeps the lady off her feet and onto the back of his horse. Like Caesar, he came he saw and he swiftly conquered. All the lady does is make a 'sweet moan' and 'sing'.

Before becoming entrapped by La Belle Dame, the knight makes her presents, love tokens of a 'garland' and a 'bracelet' and, despite her saying nothing, he confidently reads her looks as showing 'she did love'. There's a subtly disturbing, ambiguous quality to 'and sure in language strange she said'. If the language is 'strange', or foreign, how can he be 'sure' of what she is really saying?

The sixth stanza begins the reversal in power. Agency of the verbs switches to La Belle Dame. The knight becomes their passive object. He is lulled into being the submissive partner:

- 'she found me'
- 'she took me'
- 'she lulled me'

Fed and 'lulled' to sleep, he is further unmanned and diminished by being infantilised. Only in his unquiet dream does he escape the enchantment. Even here he is a passive witness rather than active agent. Significantly, Keats uses the same verb to forge a link between the knight and the narrator. Both see pale victims of La Belle Dame, both are warned of her seductive, but treacherous beauty.

Imagination, in the form of a dream, warns the knight of his fate as another victim of the mysterious enchantress. When he wakes the 'elfin grot' has disappeared and he is alone on a hill. <u>What would you do in this situation?</u> Run as fast as your legs would take you, back to battle and the manly world of knights, I warrant. <u>Warned, why then doesn't this knight escape?</u> For one thing he seems to have lost his 'pacing steed' and is now on foot. Clearly this symbolises a loss of status and masculine power. Though he appears to be alive, he also seems trapped by his experience, doomed to repeat it as a story. Or perhaps he's so pale and haggard, so withered because now this knight is now just a ghost, unable to leave the place where he lost his life.

La Belle Dame

Unless, rather perversely, we take the narrator to be female, the poem is told entirely from a male perspective. Notably, La Belle Dame Sans Merci never has the chance to express her opinions, or to explain her motivation. Her voice is silenced. <u>Who, or what, is this beautiful 'faery' woman?</u>

We know some key things about her appearance: she's 'full beautiful', with 'long' hair and 'wild' eyes. Keats emphasises this last feature through repetition of the same adjective in stanza eight, 'her wild, wild eyes'. The woman is characterised only through the vague generalities of her physical attractiveness and her untamed otherness. We learn that she's also exotic, non-human, supernatural in some way; 'a faery's child' she lives in an 'elfin grot'. Her home is away from towns and people, somewhere in the wild ['the meads']. Her appearance suggests a lost damsel from a Romance story. Initially she's docile and virtually mute, just making 'sweet' moans. And she seems extraordinarily easily wooed. All it takes is a few 'garlands' and she's ready to be whisked off on the knight's horse; hardly the behaviour of a civilised lady of virtue. Her virtual silence and easy compliance with the knight's wishes seem to make her more attractive to him. From his male perspective she's a perfect fantasy woman. The knight hardly has to do anything to persuade this beautiful woman to leap into his arms. Peculiarly, when she gets the knight home to her 'grot' she just cries and 'sigh'd full sore'. How are we to read this weeping? Regret at what she is going to do? Regret that, like the knight, she is trapped in this narrative pattern? Or are her tears meant to signal her deceitfulness? Vulnerability a subtle weapon to make the knight lower his guard even further?

Sweet tooth

After seeming entirely submissive at first, suddenly La Belle Dame takes control. She feeds the knight, as if fattening him up with tasty, exotic, heavenly food - 'relish sweet', 'honey wild' and 'manna dew'. The food can also have another symbolic significance. According to the critic, Lionel Trilling, 'for Keats, the luxury of food is connected with, and in a sense gives place to, the luxury of sexuality'. In other words, eating fruit is coded reference to sexual intercourse. If we accept this, then the poem dramatizes Keats's fear that love and intercourse might lead to some sort of entrapment and loss of male power. And in this reading, the lady behaves with a liberty that would have been deeply shocking to a polite nineteenth century audience. Then she sends him to sleep. Here she takes on the role of a mother, feeding and putting a child to bed. Does this make La Belle Dame more disconcerting? A fairy lover/ goddess/ enchantress, but also a demon/ inverted mother/ witch figure.

The phrase 'in thrall' signals that she has made the knight her slave or servant, diminishing him even further. We also learn that many men have been victims and that she has a name: La Belle Dame Sans Merci. Can we presume she must be French? Either the whole poem is set in France [but the characters fortunately speak English] or else she is French and foreign to the knight. Perhaps this adds to her impression of exotic otherness. Written not long after England had been at War with France, La Belle Dame's Frenchness might also make her seem a more threatening or symbolic figure. Clearly the repetition of the adjective 'pale', used about both the knight and the other 'pale…death-pale' victims, indicates that they have lost blood. In this sense, La Belle Dame seems to be some sort of Gothic blood-sucker, a vampire, perhaps; beautiful, predatory, deadly. That would fit with her hard-to-categorise quality. Whatever symbolic significance we assign her, she remains a fictional version of Fanny Brawne.

Unmasking La Belle Dame

More metaphorically, she could be a personification of death, or disease. Bringing 'fever' and 'anguish', weakness and 'paleness', she leaves her victim listless and forlorn [and perhaps also dead!]. Arguably she is a symbol for the irresistible power of tuberculosis, the disease that killed Keats and several

members of his immediate family. Some critics have also suggested she could symbolise drug addiction; we know that at one point during his illness Keats's friends were appalled to find he had been dosing himself with laudanum.

More radically still she could be read as a symbol of imagination, beauty or even of poetry itself. The manly knight falls in love with the woman and turns a melancholy, emasculated poet! Alas! Certainly, Keats sometimes worried that imaginative adventure, the intoxication of poetry, might be a way of avoiding engaging properly and actively with the real world. In this interpretation, La

Belle Dame is the goddess muse of poetry who enchants and enslaves the will of the male poet.

Or if we go back to her Frenchness, La Belle Dame could symbolise the revolutionary ideas that drove the French Revolution. Many of the Romantic poets were captivated by these ideas and some championed the cause of revolution - Wordsworth and Blake were notable enthusiasts. However, the aftermath of the revolution was bloody and chaotic, as one form of tyranny was replaced by another just as virulent. During the 'Reign of Terror' thousands of people were publicly executed and hopes for a better, fairer, more just society were swept away by a rising tide of blood-letting.

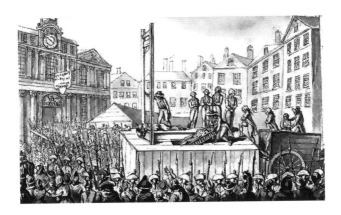

All these readings are plausible. The remarkable thing with symbols is they can pack in many meanings inside one image – and still retain their mystery. It is part of what makes Keats's poem so captivating.

A poetic spell

Keats's poem doesn't just describe an enchantment; it weaves its own spell on the reader. Mainly this is achieved through setting, repetition, adaptation of the ballad form and the poem's overall structure. The setting is sketched in a few quick strokes:

'The sedge has wither'd from the lake

and no birds sing'

A tense and eerie atmosphere is conjured by the silence and we may wonder why no birds are singing - a notorious sign of danger. The verb, 'withered' suggests decay and links the landscape to the knight on whose cheek a 'fading rose/ fast withereth too'. Keats uses pathetic fallacy here so that the landscape seems to reflect the knight's mood and mindset. As with the narrator and other dead men, this device suggests more is at stake than the fate of a single knight.

With one exception, the conjunction 'and' is used in every stanza. Sentences are organised in a simple narrative fashion: This happened and then this happened and then this happened. The absence of subordinating conjunctions indicates that Keats does not explain the events, just sets them out before us, so that they retain their mystery. The gently insistent repetition of diction, syntax, and metre establishes an incantatory rhythm. The pulse is also muted - there are few emphatically stressed syllables. The repetition of the muted rhythm further enhances the trance-like feel. Each stanza ends with a full stop and follows the same pattern. Hence, though the story moves onwards, there is a counter force of stillness and stasis.

Keats also adapts the ballad metre. Conventionally a ballad is written in quatrains of alternating four beat [tetrameters] and three beats [trimeters] often in iambic feet. The poet stretches the second lines into tetrameter: 'Alone and palely loitering'; 'So haggard and so woebegone'; 'With anguish moist and fever dew'.

Ti-TUM ti-TUM ti-TUM ti-TUM

And he docks a beat from the fourth lines. Look, for example, at 'and no birds sing', 'and made sweet moan', 'on the cold hill's side', which all end heavily with three stressed monosyllables in a row. At other times, he trims the last line of the quatrain back further: 'with kisses four', 'hath thee in thrall', 'a faery's song' are dimeters – just two beats. The unbalancing, stretching and cutting of the form creates tension at the end of each stanza, a feeling of being brought up short, or something being not quite right or as expected. Another way of thinking of the metre is in terms of rising and falling. Traditionally the second line has the falling quality of a trimeter following a tetrameter. By lengthening this line Keats has three lines with a rising quality, hence accentuating the dying fall of the final line of each stanza.

Overall the poem has a cyclical structure, with the last stanza's language echoing the first two. This link between the start and end highlights the interesting passage of time in the poem. The first two stanzas and the final one are in the present tense, 'ail', 'loitering', whereas the story the knight tells is in the past tense, 'I met', 'her hair was'. It is almost as if after the knight has told his story we re-enter the same moment, as he answers the narrator's question. Working together the various aspects conjure a feeling of suspended animation, of time stuck, held and halted, which further strengthens the poem's hypnotic, haunting spell.

La Belle crunched:

KNIGHT-AT-ARMS – ALONE – WITHER'D – NO – AIL – WOEBEGONE – FULL – DONE – LILY – FEVER – FADING – WITHERETH – LADY – FAERY'S – HAIR – EYES – GARLAND – FRAGRANT – LOVE – MOAN – STEED – NOTHING – SING – FAERY'S – RELISH – MANNA – STRANGE – TRUE – ELFIN – WEPT – WILD – KISSES – LULLED – WOE – DREAM'D – COLD – PRINCES – DEATH-PALE – BELLE – THRALL – STARVED – WARNING – AWOKE – HILL – SOJOURN – ALONE – WITHER'D – SING

NB

Perhaps we have overstated one reading; that the knight has been trapped and possibly even killed by the La Belle Dame. Another possibility is that he is so pale and feverish because he feels guilt at what has happened in the 'elfin grot'. Perhaps La Belle Dame is more innocent that we'd supposed, perhaps she is even the victim.

Alice Walker, *Poem at 39*

Remembering, relationships, regrets

How do we make sense of grief? What role do our upbringing and memories play in shaping who we are today? What mixed emotions do we feel when remembering a lost loved one? Alice Walker's *Poem at 39* presents her heartfelt memories of her father and their past relationship. The poem is touchingly emotive in its simplicity, its language reflecting the poet's deep and mixed emotions and the use of free verse [perhaps an embodiment of the influential Modernist stream of consciousness] structurally engaging the reader in Walker's flowing thought processes. Walker also deliberately also structures her poem in a way to reflect a clear shift in tone: initially she conveys some regret about the lost time that she and her father could have shared together in her childhood, yet transitions into a more optimistic nostalgia as her first-person narrative continues, reflecting the pride her father would have felt about the woman she grew up to become. Walker celebrates the range of memories that she holds as well as the similarities she notices between their two characters. Her poem thus explores the relationship between life and death, capturing the fluctuating emotions experienced during the process of remembrance.

The high price of love

Walker's initial regret of how 'tired' her father was soon gives way to more detailed memories. The poem's second verse focuses on her father's influence on her own attitude to money. She hints that he may have faced financial struggles and, consequently, hoped his daughter would learn from his mistakes and not face similar hardships. When  she says 'I learned to see/ bits of paper/ as a way/ to escape/ the life he knew' the abstract 'bits of paper' suggests a nostalgic recollection of her initially childlike approach to money, with the isolated verb 'escape' a reminder to the reader perhaps of the more challenging times they have faced and hoped to leave behind. In addition, by isolating 'account' at the end of the stanza, Walker suggests a single-minded focus on money that she learned from her father. Through the reflective tone of Walker's first person structure she reflects how, as an adult, she still cannot complete even the simplest of tasks without being reminded of her father's influence; 'I think of him' is emotive in its simplicity, the use of present tense a reminder of her father's continued influence and permanence in her memories.

There is also, arguably, deeper metaphorical significance embedded within this second stanza, beyond her father's literal influence on her approach to finances. Walker uses the imagery of money to reflect the influence her father had in her approach to life more widely: 'This is the form/ he must have said:/ the way it is done'. The 'form', on the surface, refers to her financial transactions, conveying his influence in her own understanding of managing money. However, 'form' is also a homonym: Walker could also mean 'form' to mean method or custom, and thus this may denote her father's impact on her overall outlook on the 'way' to live life. However, the tense includes a note of hesitation – 'he must have said' – implies a regret that she cannot remember his words of advice as intricately as she would wish as well as perhaps her awareness that her adult 'form' and lifestyle differed from his understanding and expectations.

Honesty is the best policy

Of course, Walker's father taught her many lessons beyond saving money. Her third stanza, in the heart of the poem, focuses on his important emotional influence, as she describes the necessity of being an honest person. The alliterative 'He taught me /that telling the truth' highlights the significance of this lesson and its influence on her later life. Walker repeats the abstract noun 'truth' later in the stanza – although, deliberately, its second reiteration is in the plural form, as she becomes aware that 'many of my truths /must have grieved him /before the end'. Again, Walker is precise in her choice of tense and the conditional 'must have', signifies that she has had to infer this in her

remembrance, without knowing his feelings as a definite fact. Whatever he truly thought, tactfully her father did not voice this grief. The poem is filled with mixed emotions and this example hints at her father's pensive character. Not wanting to hamper her development as both a child and an adult, he may have kept certain negative thoughts and opinions to himself. The verb 'grieved', in particular, reinforces Walker's recognition that she may have made decisions in life and writing which caused him unhappiness or, at least, uncertainty [particularly her homosexual feelings, having, for example, a long-term relationship with the singer-songwriter Tracy Chapman].

As a leading feminist and activist in the Civil Rights Movement, honesty was central to Walker's own values and life, a quality that she attributes to her father and her upbringing. The personification of 'truths' indicates how significant this life lesson was in shaping their relationship and her future identity. Despite any differences in her lifestyle to the way she was brought up, she positively attributes her firm belief in the importance of honesty to her father.

Like father, like daughter

Walker's repetition of the simple and direct 'How I miss my father' expresses the poem's development from regretting any lost opportunities to make the most of each other's company to a more optimistic exclamation of how proud she is of her father and the fact that she can see the connections between them. The exclamation mark after the second 'How I miss my father!' neatly embodies the poem's increasingly positive tone, as she is certain he would 'admire' her adult self. Her delight in their similar personalities is reflected in descriptions of their hobbies, particularly through the imagery of food in the penultimate stanza. The mirroring internal rhyme, 'Now I cook and look just like him', symbolises the sense of 'twoness' and harmony that she now feels. Just like the verbs 'cook' and 'look' themselves, joined together in their similar sounds and appearance, Walker and her father are wonderfully alike. The poet turns this literal comparison into a more poignant metaphor, ensuring that she is 'seasoning none of my life/ the same way twice'. Slant rhyme is used effectively here - the joining of 'life' and 'twice' connotes the unity of father and daughter and perhaps, on a deeper level, suggests that the life he lived is now being lived 'twice', as she shares so many of his traits and hobbies. In addition, 'seasoning' signifies the very 'spices' [or in other words, spontaneity and vibrancy] of her own life, influenced by her own father's implied vivacious attitude during her upbringing. He was, after all, a man who 'cooked like a person/ dancing'.

Nevertheless, this simile contrasts with the following line, the energetic implications of 'dancing' conflicting with his 'yoga meditation'. This reminds the reader of the dual sides to her father's character as well as her understandably confused and mixed feelings as she reflects on his life. The fact that Walker extends her cooking imagery across two stanzas, though, reinforces her celebration of their similarities: her 'brain light' at the fact she cooks like him not only illustrates the mindfulness of cooking but also the positive emotions she now has when considering her father's influence on her adult life.

Walker's appreciation for her father's generosity becomes increasingly apparent as the poem continues. She admires how he 'craved the voluptuous/ sharing/ of good food', the structurally isolated verb emphasising its importance, with the 'good food' not only showing his insistence that his family be cared for but representing too the shared good times that Walker spent with her father and family.

Getting to know Walker's world

Alice Walker was the youngest of eight children, born to poor parents who refused to set their children working, instead ensuring they got an education – quite a feat in the racist and sexist culture of mid twentieth century America. The financial challenges of Walker's upbringing are apparent throughout the poem, as is her emphasis on the importance of education, shown through lexis such as 'taught' and 'learned'. Her father wished his children 'to escape/ the life he knew', reflecting his deep love and care that Walker, along with her siblings, would not face the discrimination and financial hardship that so affected his generation and his outlook on life.

Alice Walker is most famous for her powerful prizewinning novel, *The Color Purple*, a novel that heavily but honestly criticises her contemporary patriarchal black society, a society that unfairly objectified women and was rife with racial and gender inequality. Walker wrote *Poem at 39* shortly after the controversial publication of *The Color Purple* and perhaps concern over how her father would have viewed her novel hovers in the poem's background. Without doubt he was, one of the most significant influences in her own life. He died just as her career was taking off and Walker's focus on truth telling ['my truths must have grieved him'] suggests the mixed feelings he may have had about her bold, feminist writing. The fact he 'grieved' at some of her truths may also refer to her sexuality, favouring female relationships rather than the heteronormative ideal of a husband and perhaps the unsentimental frankness with which she presents society. In mid twentieth century American South, honesty about both subjects would have been particularly challenging, with such embedded narrow societal ideas about gender, class and race.

However, the final triple, 'cooking, writing, chopping wood', concludes the poem on a note of celebration. The three verbs remind the reader of Walker's proud independence and they demonstrate her self-assurance in the importance of writing, the verb placed structurally at the heart of the tricolon. To Walker, writing was not only her career but her central form of self-expression, allowing her to express her remembrance and share with the reader her certainty that her father would 'admire' the fearless, truth-speaking person she has become.

Poem at 39 Crunch:

MISS – WISH – TIRED – I – BORN – WRITING – THINK – TAUGHT – FORM – SAID – LEARNED – BITS – WAY – ESCAPE – LIFE – SCHOOL – SAVINGS – ACCOUNT – TAUGHT – TRUTH – MEANING – BEATING – TRUTHS – GRIEVED – END – MISS – PERSON – DANCING – MEDITATION – CRAVED – SHARING – FOOD – LOOK – LIGHT – THIS – POT – LIFE – TWICE – STRAYS – GROWN – ADMIRE – BECOME – WRITING – FIRE

Carol Ann Duffy, *War Photographer*

In a famously distressing photograph from the Vietnam War a group of children are pictured running towards the camera and away from a napalm attack that has left the background of the photo a blaze of fire and smoke. [Napalm was an anti-personal weapon, a flammable liquid that stuck to the skin when it ignited.] To the left in the foreground a young boy's distraught expression conveys the horror and trauma of the attack. In the middle, a young, naked girl runs towards us, crying. She is clearly terrified and in agony, with napalm burns all over her body. Her burns were so bad doctors did not think she could possibly survive. Thankfully she did.

Imagine you are the photographer who took this picture. Whilst it might be a natural human instinct to immediately run to the aid of this young girl, it is your job to document these events as they unfold and report them as a neutral observer. Could you do a job like this, which requires you to suppress your empathy for the suffering of others? The image had far reaching consequences; the Western world were brought face-to-face with the devastating effect of Napalm on innocent civilians, and it helped fuel public opinion against the Vietnam war. The use of such a weapon is now against international law.

Carol Ann Duffy was inspired to write *War Photographer* due to her friendship with two well respected war photographers, Don McCullin and Philip Jones Griffiths. She was interested in the difficulties these men faced when they witnessed such horrific moments in human history and were forced to attempt to capture them for the 'consumption' of the media in the Western world. Whilst the Vietnam image may have inspired a public outcry in 1972, Duffy explores the notion that our sympathy for those depicted is fleeting, and the proliferation of images of war-torn nations has ultimately desensitised all or us to the extent that we simply 'do not care'.

The observer & the observed

Duffy has chosen to use a third person narrative perspective throughout, creating the impression that 'The War Photographer' of the title is the subject under scrutiny. There is a clear irony here, as the observer becomes the observed; the poetic voice scrutinises the intimate moments of the photographer in his dark room, revealing his inner turmoil as he 'is finally alone'.

The intimate knowledge the narrator has of the photographer's thoughts gives the reader the impression that the photographer's mind is turning inwards; he appears to be scrutinising his role in creating these 'spools of suffering' - the sibilance here perhaps reinforcing his sense of disgust. The fragmented sentence structures are like a stream of consciousness: 'Belfast. Beirut. Phnom Penh', as if his mind is flashing back to the war-torn locations almost involuntarily.

Ordinary pain

The sequence of flashbacks is brought to life with the final sentence of the first stanza 'all flesh is grass'. This is a much-quoted biblical phrase used to refer to the transitory nature of life: ultimately when we die our flesh is returned to the earth and feeds in to the cycle of life. Used in this context the image could reflect the way the photographer is attempting to comfort himself and rationalise the immense quantity of death he is witnessing. The reference to 'flesh' could refer to the nakedness of the victims (linking to the picture of the Vietnam girl); their indignity overwhelms him and covers the images quite literally like a landscape of grass. Reminding himself of this saying is an example of the way he attempts to separate his own emotional responses from what he is witnessing, but this becomes increasingly difficult as the poem progresses.

There is a juxtapositioning throughout the poem of the suffering experienced by the people in the war-torn communities and the mundane lives of those in 'Rural England'. Statements such as 'simple weather can dispel' our 'ordinary pain' and that the 'fields' of England don't 'explode beneath the feet of running children' emphasise the gulf between experiences. We take the peace and security of our land for granted, and the image of running children is particularly powerful in evoking a sense of the vulnerability and innocence of many of those caught up in these war zones. Once again, the Vietnam image of the running girl is evoked, particularly within the last phrase of the stanza: 'nightmare heat' with its suggestions of napalm. Coupled with the reference to flesh in the last phrase of the opening stanza, we cannot fail to make the connection with the burning skin of children. Duffy's use of imagery combined with careful structuring is hugely powerful and evocative, bringing home to the reader both what the civilians in battlegrounds experience, and how the war photographer struggles to cope with bearing witness to it.

Trembling & control

Duffy adopts the traditional iambic pentameter throughout most the poem, a metre often reserved for weighty and serious topics. However, there are key moments where she deviates from the pattern. Line two of stanza one, for example, contains an additional iamb, reflecting how the 'spools of suffering' are too great to be contained within the line. The line therefore becomes iambic hexameter, also known as an alexandrine. In line four of stanza one the opposite happens; only four iambs are used. In contrast to the over-spilling of suffering in line two, Duffy here could be highlighting the inadequacy the photographer feels his dark room offers as a place of sanctity to develop these images of the end of human life.

The four regular stanzas each consisting of exactly six lines reflect the photographer's desire to maintain order and control over his emotions. This idea is further evident in the 'ordered rows' he uses to lay out his images. The rhyme scheme is also regular, with a rhyming couplet in lines two and three and five and six of each stanza. However, the fact that lines one and four do not tie in with this neat, ordered pattern reflects that despite his best efforts, the photographer is not able to fully maintain regimented control, over suffering, over his emotions and over the effect of his photos. This ties in with the 'tremble' that creeps into his hands, as he attempts to remind himself that 'he has a job to do.'

The second stanza starts abruptly. A matter of fact tone is swiftly established,  as the photographer attempts to jolt his mind back to the more mundane tasks of the present, where 'solutions slop in trays'. Again, however, the sibilance which creeps into this phrase highlights his disgust, and reveals the trembling of his hands. This time as he thinks of the present, the sentence fragment 'Rural England' also carries a sense of distaste, perhaps even bitterness. 'Home again' follows. Any comfort is, however very short-lived. Just a couple of metrical beats later and his mind turns to the contrast between the 'ordinary pain' felt here with the suffering felt by the 'running children' who are the subjects of his photographs.

The start of the third stanza contrasts with the start of the second. Whereas at that point he had been attempting to force himself to focus on the task at hand, this time the statement 'Something is happening' demonstrates that he has now been irrevocably drawn into the world of his photographs. The development of the photographs is of course what the photographer is aiming to do, but the process of the development of one picture in particular absorbs him completely; whilst the subject of the picture is a 'stranger' to him (the phrase perhaps highlighting the attitude he typically takes towards his subjects), the way in which he becomes a 'half-formed ghost' reflects the ghostly nature of the image, and hints towards the fact that he is no longer alive. This is confirmed as his mind turns to 'the cries of this man's wife' and how the 'blood stained into the foreign dust'.

They do not care

The final stanza acts as a moment of realisation for the war photographer; the pain of a single man in the previous stanza merge into 'a hundred agonies', emphasising that the shot he captured is a drop in the ocean of suffering he witnesses. Emotive language is juxtaposed with the more factual 'in black and white', bringing us to the perspective of his editor who merely sees the images as a product he is packaging for consumption within 'Sunday's supplement' of his paper. There is a bitterness in the subsequent reference to the reader's response, as although their 'eyeballs prick with tears', this is a fleeting moment quickly forgotten as they move on to their comfortable lives and their 'pre-lunch beers'. The trite internal rhyme reinforces the sense of the photographer's disdain. The narrative perspective finally brings us back to the point of view of the photographer who gazes 'impassively', emotionally disconnected, out of the aeroplane window at his own country where 'they do not care' about his work nor the suffering he is paid to witness for us.

War Photographer crunched:

FINALLY – SUFFERING – RED – CHURCH – PRIEST – FLESH – JOB – TREMBLE – HOME – DISPEL – EXPLODE – NIGHTMARE – HAPPENING – TWIST – GHOST – APPROVAL – MUST – BLOOD – AGONIES – EDITOR – SUPPLEMENT – BEERS – IMPASSIVELY – CARE.

William Blake, *The Tyger*

The fool and the wise man see not the same tree

There have been many different competing interpretations of Blake's poem since it first appeared in his extraordinary book *Songs of Innocence and Experience* [1793]. If you're a teacher, you could give the class the poem and ask them to come up with as many different interpretations as possible in ten

teacher timed minutes, or you could ask them in pairs to choose the most persuasive from a list of interpretations. Once they have made their choice, each pair could have ten teacher timed minutes to amass evidence to support their reading in preparation for discussion or debate with other

pairs. Make this as co-operative or competitive an exercise as you deem fit. If the latter, you could devise a point scoring system with yourself as the incorruptible umpire, perhaps. If you're a student, you can do a similar exercise now within the debate chamber of your brain. Consider each of the following interpretations of Blake's poem, decide which one you find most convincing, or perhaps, most interesting, re-read the poem and select evidence you'd cite to convince yourself of this interpretation. Start off thinking like a barrister who must persuade a sceptical jury and an intimidatingly intellectual and stern judge. Then switch roles and be that rigorous judge. How good was the evidence? Once you've finished reading this essay and when you're revising *The Tyger* for your examination you may want to follow the same exercise with each of these interpretations. If you do this with an open mind, you might even change your interpretation.

Interpretation #1: This is simply an animal poem, one in which the awestruck poet brilliantly imagines the fearsomeness of an apex predator.

Interpretation #2: Quite wrong, I'm afraid: The poem is a religious one, it's real subject being the nature of God and his creation. In particular, the poet wrestles with the existence of evil; hence all the fire imagery.

Interpretation #3: Piffle and poppycock: This is a poem about the fiery and irrepressible powers of the imagination, hammered into shape by art.

Interpretation #4: How naive and egocentric! Art about the nature of art. Actually, this is a poem about the Industrial Revolution and its effects upon the working classes. It is a warning, like Shelley's *Frankenstein* of a monster being forged in the factories and mills of England.

Interpretations #5: You Marxists, so predictable. Can't you see that this is a masculinist poem expressing admiration for powerful and violent forces in nature, in society and in *man*kind?

Interpretation #6: Utter rot, complete hogwash. No, no and thrice no. This is a fundamentally political poem in coded, symbolic language. What it's really about is the French Revolution. That tiger? = Revolutionary.

Putting interpretation aside for a while, the qualities that make Blake's poem so striking and memorable are entirely poetic. The vibrancy of the poem is generated, in particular, by its metre, rhyme pattern, diction and imagery.

Take the first line, for instance. This sets up the mood, tone, atmosphere, sound world and rhythm of the poem. And it starts off at quite a lick:

'Tiger, tiger, burning bright'

Firstly, it's very concise, just four words and only seven syllables. The eye gets to the end of the first line quickly and drops down to the next one. Secondly the metre is very distinctive. A more conventional opening would be an iambic, unstress/ stress, one; Blake's switch to trochaic, stress/ unstress, signals right from the get-go that he's going to be approaching his subject in a different way. So, the line starts with a stress and it also ends with one on 'bright'. Blake has either docked the first unstressed syllable from the start or

the end of the line. Consider more standard alternatives: 'The tiger, tiger, burning, bright,' or 'tiger, tiger, burning brightly'. Clearly Blake's version is more intense, more concentrated, more stressy and more muscular. Any redundant words or even
syllables have been cut away, making the line lean, mean and memorable. I said 'stressy' and what I meant was that Blake manages to include more stressed than unstressed syllables, four to three [stresses are in bold] and hence the metre goes from strong, i.e. stressed, to strong:

'**Tig**er, **tig**er, **bur**ning **bright**'

It's an emphatic, thumping rhythm. The word choices and sound qualities of the words contribute significantly to the effect. As well as the obvious repetition of the first word and tight alliteration, a few sounds dominate the line:

- Assonance of the open 'i' of 'tiger' and 'bright'

- The opening and closing 't' in 'tiger' and 'bright'
- The 'grr/ brr' sound linking 'tiger' to 'burning' and 'bright'

Add to that, the diction and imagery. Simply the word 'tiger' conjures up powerful images that, for example the word 'twinkle' does not. The fact that it is repeated creates emphasis, of course, but also suggests a kind of doubletake. This creature is so incredible, especially to a Londoner like Blake in the eighteenth century that he has to say it twice to believe it. Then there is the image of fire, with its vibrant orange colour, its energy and danger, and the burning is intense and vivid, 'bright'.

It's the combination of these various aspects, metre, sonic devices, diction, imagery that conjure such potency in the line. If you need convincing, compare the metrically identical: 'twinkle, twinkle, little star'. Not quite the same effect, we hope you'll agree.

Blake's use of couplets adds to the pounding, muscular qualities of the verse. But having set up the percussive rhythm in the first three lines, the poem then stumbles in the last line of the opening quatrain. This happens because 'try' rhymes with 'eye', tripping the reader up by the rhyme's appearance earlier in the line than we expect and on a relatively insignificant, metrically unstressed word. Moreover, that rhyme only emphasises the fact that the end-rhyme word, 'symmetry' doesn't rhyme properly with 'eye'. Unless that is we contort the word's normal stress pattern and pronunciation to produce '**symm**-et-**try**' with an 'i' rather than 'ee' sound at the end. But that doesn't work. And now that our ear has brought our attention to this word it seems rather out-of-place in a poem about a tiger. Symmetry is an architectural or mathematical word that doesn't sit naturally with 'tigers', 'burning', 'night', 'forests' or 'fearfulness'. Perhaps it might belong with 'frame'. But, in any case, how exactly can symmetry be 'fearful'? Those are two words that don't belong together and in any other case, how exactly Mr. Blake, is a tiger symmetrical? So, we're only on the last line of the first stanza and already things have become pretty weird in Blake's poem.

What the?

The second stanza continues with a double perspective. The poem explores two ideas at once; the nature of the tiger and that of its creator. If you know your classical literature you'll recognise the image of seizing the fire as an allusion to the Prometheus myth. In brief Prometheus stole the divine fire from Mount Olympus and gave it to man. For his troubles, Zeus had him bound to a rock where Prometheus's stomach was pecked out each day by a giant eagle. He's looking a bit healthier in the picture on the right [and he was obviously also very nifty with the arrangement of his billowing cape] but Prometheus  suffered horrifically for helping humankind. So, the creator of the tiger, the hand that seized the fire, is not like Zeus, but rather a rebellious titan who feels sympathy for poor, dumb, brutish humans. How could this be reconciled with a Christian reading of *The Tyger*?

Emphatic repetitions power the next two stanzas. Specifically, 'and what', 'what', 'heart' and 'dread' are repeated numerous times. Progressively the lines get shorter as the barrage of questions grow more urgent. The shortest question is just three words, 'what the chain?' A number of critics have suggested that all those 'whats' sound some sort of thumping or hammering as if Blake is bashing at the doors of perception, trying to understand the savage phenomenon of the tiger and its even more powerful creator. At times the two characters, creator and created, seem indistinguishable in the din of the poem. Grammatically, either of them, for instance, could be subject of 'what dread hand? And what dread feet'. References to 'hammers', 'chains', 'furnace' and 'anvil' imply that the tiger is created out of metal by a blacksmith or ironsmith. And it is this titanic, Vulcan-like figure that is the really 'dread' one, clasping the 'deadly terrors' of the tiger. Though Blake was a devout Christian, albeit a non-conformist one, the iconography here doesn't appear Christian, the creator god of this poem, doesn't seem to be the Christian God.

Curiously, the following image does appear to be Christian, an allusion, perhaps, to the rebellion in heaven in which Satan was defeated and hurled down into hell. It prompts the question of how the creator might feel about his work. Another way of phrasing this would be was God pleased by this outcome, even though, as He is omniscient He already knew it would happen? Here Blake seems to be gnawing away at the age-old problem of evil and its existence despite God's supposed omniscience and omnipotence. The idea is picked up in the following key question: 'Did he who made the lamb make thee?'

Songs of Innocence and Experience features correspondences between poems in its two halves, so that a poem in Innocence is coupled with one in Experience. As the title suggests, the innocent poem often presents its subject through a child-like perspective. Sometimes this perspective is pure and almost saintly, at other times it can seem a little naive, even ignorant. The matching experience poem often offers a sort of corrective, a darker, more grown-up take on the subject. We should not, however, assume the innocent view is mistaken and the experienced one  correct; rather for Blake the truth arrives, like the book of poetry itself, out of a synthesis of the two contrary views. The corresponding poem to *The Tyger* is, of course, called *The Lamb*. It's a sweet little poem in which a child narrator looks at a lamb [a Christian symbol for Christ, of course] and surmises that as God created the lamb, God must be like a lamb. Clearly this child would have an awful fright if he came across the tiger. By the child's logic, God would have to be tiger-like. So, did the same god create the gentle, meek and mild lamb and the fiery fierce terror of the tiger? If so, why did he create the latter? If the lamb = Christ, does the tiger = Satan?

Blake's poem doesn't give us answers. In total there are fourteen questions in its six stanzas; which is an awful lot of questions. They imply and urgent need for answers to huge, fundamental questions about the nature of the world and its creator.

Republic of tigers?

0What of the other interpretations? Well, there's another creator in this poem, the poet. Not only 'could' he frame the 'tiger', he also dares to do it. He wrestles the deadly terror into the bars of lines and the prisons of his quatrains and he restrains its energies in rhyme. Or rather, with its emphatic, pounding rhythms isn't this poem more like an incantation, a spell to conjure the spirit of the tiger and its even more dreadful creator? French revolutionaries were sometimes referred to in the English press as tigers for their alleged savagery and the terror they unleashed on the streets of Paris. In this reading, the 'forests of the night' refer to the benighted streets of the French capital, burning with revolution. What possible force could or dare contain or frame the outbreak of anarchic violence? Switch Paris to London and revolutionaries to the working classes, beaten and bashed into monstrous shape by the forces of the Industrial Revolution, and you arrive at a different version of a socio-political reading. Perhaps that word, 'symmetry' that puzzled us can be explained by this reading - there is a symmetry between the violence inflicted on a society by an oppressive government and the vengeful violence that will break out as a reaction. Certainly, the symmetry appears to be more about the relation between the poem's major two figures, the tiger and its creator, rather than an aspect of the former. After all, Blake's

own illustration for the poem, shown here, presents the big cat side-on, where there is no possible symmetry. A recent biographer of Blake, Peter Acroyd, comments on this  image that Blake's tiger is about as terrifying as a 'stuffed toy' and is 'ludicrously comic'.[3] Certainly, the creature is wearing a rather self-satisfied

---

[3] Ackroyd, *Blake*, pp. 143-146

and rather enigmatic smile. Perhaps only this tyger knows what it really symbolises.

The Tyger crunched:

TIGER - NIGHT - IMMORTAL - SYMMETRY - DISTANT - FIRE - ASPIRE - DARE - ART - SINEWS - HEART - DREAD - HAMMER - WHAT - FURNACE - ANVIL - CLASP - SPEARS - TEARS - SMILE - LAMB - BURNING - FORESTS - IMMORTAL - DARE

NB

Personally, for me, Blake's poem can only be fully explained by applying extensive knowledge of the rest of his poetry and, in particular, the radical poet's radical re-writing of the whole story of creation. To do this, Blake felt

compelled to create his own mythological characters, including figures he called the four 'Zoahs'. One of these 'Zoahs', called 'Orc', to our left, is a figure of dynamic fiery

and creative energy. Blake often depicts another of the Zoahs, Los, with a hammer and anvil and he seems to be the spirit of poetic imagination. A fourth Zoah, Urizen [depicted reading his iron laws, above] is the presiding god of Blake's age; he is a stern, unbending, controlling figure with iron laws. Broadly then, the tiger = Orc; his promethean creator = Los and the Zeus figure = Urizen.

Robert Browning, *My Last Duchess*

Can you recognise a monster when you see one? Why of course you can; it's an essential life skill. Monsters are huge and hairy with horrible warts on their faces; they have horns on their heads and terrible claws and mouths full of spikey teeth. Monsters have wings or scales and they hiss or growl, slobber or roar, and they slither around or they scuttle, crawl or lope. Basically, monsters are amalgams of all the features we find frightening or disgusting in the animal kingdom. In short, monsters always look something like these little critters on our right of this page:

Right?
Wrong.

And we know where to find monsters too: In horror films and fairy tales, in the middle of the woods, under our beds, hiding in our cupboards, in nightmares.

Right?
Wrong.

Because make no mistake about it, though he's a Duke and fabulously wealthy and lives in a fabulous mansion, though he's highly refined and speaks impressively and fluently, though he is a connoisseur of fine art and is exactingly polite, even though we find him here in the elegant frame of this poem, this character is a monster. And monsters who disguise their monstrosity under an attractive façade are the most scary and dangerous monsters, right? Right.

Browning's poem is a superlative example of a dramatic monologue, a poem written in the voice of a character. As the name implies, a dramatic monologue is like a single speech from a play. A successful dramatic monologue will not only allow an insight into the character speaking but also suggest a wider narrative of which they are part. A key technique in a dramatic monologue is irony. The irony operates in the gap between what the speaking character is telling us and what the writer is telling us about them. In Browning's poem, we have several characters - the Duke, the Duchess, the Count's messenger as well as the implied voice of the poet himself. The reader is placed in the position of the messenger to whom our narrator, the Duke, tells us a story about his dead wife.

What makes this poem superlative? Think for a moment of the technical challenge Browning has set himself. Creating the authentic voice of the Duke would be a stiff challenge for any novelist, using prose, but Browning has got to make this voice sound natural and convincing whilst stringing it across a regular metre. More than that, he has also chosen to use the couplet form, a form which inevitably draws attention to the rhyme words. Notice how Browning arranges sentences to subdue these rhymes and you'll be on your way to appreciating the Shakespearesque skill the poet employs here. And, having mentioned the bard, one way of thinking of the Duke is as kin to Shakespeare's duplicitous villains, Iago and Claudius might spring to mind. To appreciate Browning's technical accomplishment how about writing a reply to his poem in the form of a dramatic monologue in the voice of either the Count, the Duchess or the messenger?

Never stoop

The Duke is holding court. The eloquence of his words expresses his refined aristocratic manner. A domineering character, it seems he has total control of the narrative, speaking uninterrupted for 28 couplets. From the outset, he is in command, talking at, not with, the Count's messenger, politely condescending to him. Look, for example, at how he controls the topic of conversation, or how when he asks questions he doesn't wait for or allow a reply. Showing off his house and its possessions to indicate his power, prestige and wealth, the Duke establishes his credentials as a potential husband for the Count's daughter. The references to the artists, Fra Pandolf and Claus of Innsbruck, establish his cultural credentials, but also subtly contribute to the power-play. We do not know these artists and hence we are made to feel ignorant and inferior to the knowledgeable Duke. Extraordinarily self-assured, he high-handedly assumes that we, the listening audience, agree with his opinions. He portrays himself as a connoisseur of the arts and of good breeding. Indicating that he does not tolerate those who displease him, inadvertently, however, he reveals other, much darker aspects of his character. In this crucial way, Browning exerts control over the Duke.

We learn key things about the Duke's character:

- He is obsessed with control and possession
- He is extremely proud of his family heritage 'a nine-hundred years-old name'
- He has an exacting, refined sense of good taste 'here you miss / Or there you exceed the mark'
- He is breath-takingly arrogant, 'and I choose/never to stoop' (i.e. lower himself to explain how the Duchess's behaviour offended his sensibilities and pride)
- Crucially we also learn that he was murderously possessive and pathologically jealous: 'Since none puts by/ the curtain I have drawn for you, but I'.

Evil can come dressed in fine clothes, hidden by handsome manners. Slowly we come to realise that the accomplished, authoritative, intimidating manner of the Duke hides a monstrous nature: In truth, the Duke is a cruel, vindictive, merciless man. His perverse value system raises etiquette and social snobbery above morality. Specifically, he is a man who has had his wife murdered because she was too innocent, too friendly and kind-

hearted: 'I gave commands/ Then all smiles stopped together'. And now he is turning his attention to a new potential wife who he refers to chillingly as his 'object'.

One of the most horrific aspects of the Duke's aristocratic hauteur is his refusal even to tell his dead wife how her actions so offended him. He denies her even the chance to amend her ways and so avoid her doom. He doesn't even tell her what he condemns her to death for. This is made even worse, if possible, by the fact that he refuses to inform her of what 'disgusts' him, simply because he regards this as beneath his dignity, 'I choose/ never to stoop'. It is chilling too how the Duke shows no remorse. And there is also no suggestion that he will, or could, be brought to justice for murder. Because he is a Duke he seems to be above and beyond the law. He could do with his wife as he liked because of who he was and the warped values of the society in which he lived.

The cultured impression we form of the Duke is generated by the language he uses and how he uses it. In addition to using complex vocabulary what is most striking is the Duke's syntax and sentence construction. Scan the poem quickly and you'll notice there are lots of hyphens, question marks and semicolons. In themselves, these punctuation marks suggest linguistic complexity and this is enhanced by the construction of the Duke's sentences. The longest run over nine lines, moving forward, but also halting frequently, with many clauses and parentheses, giving the impression that the fastidious Duke is trying to be very precise and exact about what he is saying. There's something sinuous to how these long sentences uncoil across lines. In stark contrast the key lines in the poem are much shorter and blunter: 'This grew; I gave commands/ Then all smiles stopped together'.

The Duke's linguistic command is also conveyed metrically. In Renaissance literature, nobility of language is often taken to express nobility of character. A regular rhythm conveys poise and control over language. Here the language moves easily and fluently forward with the character speaking the lines fully in charge of what he is saying. Here is refined and elegant articulacy. A regular pattern also gives the poet something from which to deviate. In these deviations lies significance.

Look at the section from line 29 – 43, for instance, and you will see that the pattern of the verse becomes a little less smooth and regular. Browning achieves this by extensive use of caesura and hyphens. Line 31, for instance, contains multiple pauses, small hesitations and breaks in the flow: two beats then a comma, two more, then a full stop, three more beats followed by a comma and a hyphen, one beat and an exclamation mark. The disruption is enhanced by syntax that is contorted: The clause 'I know not how' is awkwardly stuck in the middle of the sentence and the exclamatory 'good' is suddenly interjected:

'...Or blush, at least. She thanked men, - good! but thanked...'

Despite the best efforts of our will, our body language often gives away what we are really feeling. Similarly, slips in the metrical pattern betray the Duke's uncharacteristic discomposure here, the difficulty he is having maintaining his facade. Simultaneously such metrical irregularities bring these crucial lines to our closer attention.

A heart too soon made glad

Her husband describes her in a way intended to make the listener unsympathetic to the Duchess. From the Duke's haughty point of view, she

was far too free with her favour, just too friendly. But these qualities viewed negatively by the Duke may well be read as positive attributes, especially by modern readers. For example, the Duchess is shown to have an intense emotional quality: 'the depth and passion' of an 'earnest glance', and a ready capacity for happiness, ''twas not/ her husband's presence only, called that spot/ of joy into the Duchess' cheek', she had a 'heart...too soon made glad'.

She seems generous spirited, tending to 'like whate'er/ she looked on' and she is appreciative and courteous, 'she thanked men'. Whereas the Duke condemns her lack of discernment; the reader warms to her lack of snobbery and prejudice, her appreciation of simple, ordinary things: 'the dropping of the daylight...the white mule...all and each/ would draw from her alike the approving speech'. The Duke suggests that there may have been something flirtatious in her manner: 'her looks went everywhere'; we infer this perception is infected by his acute jealousy. 'Her looks went everywhere' may mean simple that she smiled at everyone.

What the Duke really cannot bear is her lack of appreciation for his aristocratic lineage: She seemed to weigh 'my gift of a nine-hundred-years-old name/ with anybody's gift'. In other words, she was not socially snobbish and did not behave as if she was superior to other people. To the Duke this behavior was an unforgivable insult to his pride and honour. So, we can conclude that the

Duke is haughty, emotionally and morally cold, as well as being supremely arrogant; the Duchess is his opposite; warm, vivacious, appreciative, charming. And for that he has her killed.

The painting of the Duchess is particularly significant. It reveals qualities of the central characters: the vivacity of the Duchess and the contrasting cold psychotic jealousy of her husband. Why is the Duke happier with the copy of the Duchess than with the real thing? Because he can control access to the painting, and because in it the Duchess is static, passive, unchanging. He views the painting and the person as possessions, the former adds to his status and esteem; alive, the Duchess detracted from it. A crucial detail is that 'Her mantle laps/ over my lady's wrist too much'. Like costumes in the theatre, dress in Renaissance paintings is very important. The mantle is the sleeve of her costume and it is a crucial, but characteristically ambiguous symbol. It suggests that there was something about the Duchess that was transgressive, 'laps over', and perhaps excessive 'too much'. In other words, in her own small way the Duchess stepped over boundaries. Of course, this quality can be viewed positively, reflecting somebody not bound by snobbish rules and regulations, someone who does not follow convention for convention's sake. But it can also be read negatively, as revealing someone who is ill mannered, who doesn't follow the correct polite behaviour. Moreover, it implies than even the very slightest non-compliance with strict rules, exceeding in some way 'the mark', will not only be noticed and frowned upon, but also severely punished.

The voice of Browning

As we have noted, the critical device used in dramatic monologues is irony. Irony undermines and transforms superficial meaning. And it is in the irony we hear the moral voice of the poet and his criticism of the values of society. Through picking up implied meaning, by reading between the lines, we hear Browning's voice behind the Duke's. For the Duke, addressing the messenger, his subject is his possessions, his house and especially his artworks. But, for Browning, addressing us, the readers, the subject is the

Duke himself. The irony works against the Duke and in favour of the Duchess: The Duke presents himself in a way he assumes to be favourable. He assumes we will agree with his worldview, his values and his behaviour. He assumes will be impressed by his grand demeanour and style. In fact, his behaviour and his values are shown to be vile and reprehensible. What he takes to be taste, we read as snobbery; what he takes to be honour, we read as selfish egotism and pride; what he presents as good breeding, we read as cold, pathological, murderous jealousy.

A noble frame

Browning's poem is one long, solid and unbroken stanza, comprising 28 rhymed couplets. If it were a building the poem would be a palace, or perhaps an elegant and well-constructed fortress. There are no breaks, or gaps or chinks of weakness in this fortress. The form of rhymed iambic couplets Browning employs is sometimes called heroic verse, a form that constitutes another part of the façade of the Duke. The elegant, noble form of heroic verse, clicking harmoniously into its repeated patterns is like expensive clothes and fine manners, hiding the fundamental monstrosity of the Duke. The poise and balance of the verse is his outer manner in action. Moreover, as Stephen Fry writes, Browning creates a 'ironic contrast between the urbane conversational manner, the psychotic darkness of the story and the elegant solidity of a noble form. The heroic verse is the frame out of which character can leap; it is itself the nobly proportioned, exquisitely tasteful palace in which ignobly misproportioned, foully tasteless deeds are done'.[4]

My Last Duchess crunched:

DUCHESS – ALIVE – WONDER – STANDS – LOOK – DESIGN – STRANGERS – EARNEST – NONE – I – SEEMED – HOW – SIR – HUSBAND'S – JOY – LAPS – TOO – FAINT – DIES – THOUGHT – JOY – HEART – EASILY – EVERYWHERE – MY – DROPPING – FOOL – MULE – ALL – APPROVING – THANKED – RANKED – GIFT –

---

[4] *The Ode Less Travelled*, p.206

ANYBODY'S – **TRIFLING** – **WILL** – **JUST** – **DISGUSTS** – **EXCEED** – **LESSONED** – **EXCUSE** – **STOOPING** – **NEVER** – **WITHOUT** – **COMMANDS** – **STOPPED** – **ALIVE** – **REPEAT** – **MASTER'S** – **PRETENSE** – **DOWRY** – **DAUGHTER'S** – **OBJECT** – **NEPTUNE** – **TAMING** – **ME**

NB

Despite the hostility of her domineering father, in 1846 Robert Browning secretly courted and married Elizabeth Barrett. A few days later the two poets escaped family and society outrage by eloping to Italy. Their shocking behaviour was condemned stridently by Elizabeth's father, who disinherited her, and by her brothers. Six years older than Robert, Elizabeth had been a recluse and was disabled; hence she did fit the convention of the perfect wife. Though Browning's poem features Renaissance characters, it is simultaneously about Victorian society and powerfully expresses a growing awareness of, and protest against, the abuse of women by patriarchal society.

John Agard, *Half-Caste*

Explain yuself wha yu mean

Recently we've had an American president who is mixed race. Turn on your TV and you'll come across many actors, presenters and sports people who are mixed race. The term 'half-caste' has almost disappeared from our language. Clearly, in many ways and in many places attitudes to race and to the mixing of different races has changed and changed for the better in the two decades since John Agard wrote this poem.

However, we should bear in mind the sometimes grim history of race relations in the twentieth century. At the start of that century, books were being written about race that argued the mixing of races would lead to a 'mongrel race of degenerates'. The Nazis believed in white racial purity and white supremacy. It wasn't until as recently as the 1960s that public segregation of races was abolished and 'miscegenation' laws repealed in the U.S.A. [Miscegenation laws criminalised close inter-racial relationships and banned marriage between  white and black people.] In South Africa there was the system of separation of races, known as apartheid, which lasted into the last decade of the twentieth century. And the term 'half-caste' was used widely in British culture until fairly recently, even though it derives from the Latin 'castus', which means pure. So 'half-caste' meant impure, corrupted, inferior. This history of ideas about race and language form the background to Agard's poem.

How many times have you heard people say 'it's political correctness gone mad'? Certainly, we hear this a lot, and many people worry that political correctness closes down proper, frank debate. Fear of being offensive, or being labelled offensive, means people can't say what they think and so debate is stifled. Or so goes the argument against political correctness. One example sometimes cited is the 'safe spaces' movement in our universities which seeks to protect students from exposure to offensive remarks and attitudes. The motivation behind this movement is laudable and its aim - for more respect for different views - is surely a good one. But, if in effect 'safe spaces' impinge on freedom of speech then they are counterproductive: Dangerous ideas and attitudes need to be challenged through open debate and discussion.

On the other hand, other than a tiny mindless minority, who now thinks it is acceptable to use offensive words like 'nigger', 'coon', 'whop, 'paki' or 'yid'? Go back to England in the 1960s, when Agard was a young man, and many of these words were commonly in use. Language influences the way we think and the way we relate to other people and it expresses our identity. Political correctness made us more aware of the ideas behind words that were once in everyday use and it made us more sensitive and respectful in our language choices. Surely that has been a good thing. Agard's poem, for example, unpacks the implications of using a once common word, a word used to classify a whole group of people and intentionally or, sometimes when used casually, inadvertently, to imply that these people were somehow inferior, second class citizens, only 'half' as good as their 'pure blood' neighbours.

I half-caste human being

Known for the electrifying and highly entertaining readings of his poetry, Agard comes from a performance poetry background and from the get-go the poet creates a keen sense of a person speaking in *Half-Caste*. Opening with the polite 'excuse me' the poem develops a conversation style with a speaker addressing an imaginary, rather ignorant, interlocutor. Agard's wry sense of humour is also immediately apparent - his speaker is standing on one leg, because as a 'half' human he might be assumed to only have one. Immediately the absurdity of thinking of anyone as 'half' is established. The polite opening modulates into something stronger in the second stanza, the imperative, 'explain yuself'. This phrase is repeated like a refrain throughout the poem, and demands that a full justification is given for the casual use of the derogatory term 'half-caste'. If the addressee is ignorant, rather than actively racist, if they're unaware of the implications of using the term, Agard will spell these implications out for them in a series of easy-to-follow examples.

He starts, however, by providing examples from art and one from nature of how mixing things together can be productive, creative and natural:

1. Picasso mixed assorted colour paints to produce his art
2. Tchaikovsky mixed black and white keys to produce music
3. English weather is produced by the mixing of 'light and shadow'.

A further implied example is, of course, the poem itself. Agard's examples highlight the absurdity of thinking that creativity comes from a principle of separation. What is metaphor, for instance, other than a connecting of things? In the second half of the poem, the focus switches to the poet himself and his listener.

Again, Agard uses humour, suggesting he will listen with 'wid de keen/ half of mih ear'. But there's a serious point behind this humour and righteous anger too. The implication of using the term 'half-caste' is to label people like Agard half-human, their capacities, abilities and worth 'half' those of other people. The poet expresses this poignantly when he refers to himself dreaming only 'half-a-dream' and casting only 'half-a-shadow'. In a final reversal, at the end of the poem, the tables are turned on the addressee. Agard implies that this person/ these people who carelessly bandy about words like 'half-caste' are not really using their own brains properly. There's something half-cocked and half-brained about their perceptions and ideas. In characteristically direct, commanding language, the poet tells his addressee[s] that they 'must come back' and use the 'whole' of their eye, ear and mind in order that they may form a better understanding of the ideas behind the words they use.

The persuasive, rhetorical nature of Agard's poem is evident in the prominent use of imperatives ['explain yuself'] and emphatic repetition, particularly in the classical pattern of threes: 'Picasso' - 'de sky' - 'Tchaikovsky'; 'listening' - 'looking' - 'offer'; 'half-a-eye' - 'half-a-dream' - 'half-a-shadow'; 'whole or yu eye/ ear / mind'.

Mash up yu grammar

Agard's poem embodies and exemplifies the rich creative fruits of inter-mixing and hybridity. In his case, the poet blends distinct types of language to create a distinct style of English dub poetry. Specifically, *Half-Caste* is written in a non-standard vernacular of phonetically spelt English that conveys an Afro-Caribbean accent. We don't need to labour the point, but characteristic non-standard spellings include, 'yuself', 'de', 'o', 'dem' and 'wid' and the phrase 'ah rass' [meaning 'my arse'] comes from the Caribbean. Verbs are also used in non-standard ways, with the simple present tense, such as 'tchaikovsky / sit down', predominant. At other times, function words are deleted. For example, 'do' from line five and 'that' from line seven. But the whole poem is not composed of non-standard English; rather it is a mash-up of standard and non-standard forms. The standard spellings include words, such as 'symphony' and 'consequently', which themselves come from Old French as well as words of Anglo-Saxon origin.

The combined effect of these choices of diction is to make the verse more immediate, leaner, punchier, more like animated speech. And the way we speak, like the words other people use about us, is a key aspect of our identities. Agard's hybrid poem is his character, his unique sense of self, rendered in colourful words. It is a linguistic celebration and assertion of the value of mixedness.

Agard is something of a rebel, a non-conformist. He's determined to go about things his own way and won't submit to the 'rules' or standards constructed by

other people. Whose 'rules', whose 'standards' are these anyway, he might ask. The same people, perhaps, who coined terms like 'half-caste'? As well as deviating from Standard English, for example, the poet creates his own poetic form, using non-standard stanzas, dispensing with metre, varying the line lengths as he pleases and eschewing capitalisation and punctuation. Other than the occasional use of a back slash /, *Half-Caste* is punctuation free. Clearly this implies connectivity; no full stops separate lines or sentences - they are all part of the same whole. The lack of a full stop at the end of the poem also ties in with the final sentiments, that the poem only provides 'half' of the story and there's more to come. Moreover, it implies the issues the poem tackles are not over and finished with, but that they continue to pervert our perceptions and relationships. Like culture, language is shaped by history and carries its historical baggage around with it. This baggage needs to be acknowledged, challenged and perhaps, sometimes, dumped on the scrap heap. Surely, it's a sign of progress, for instance, that nowadays teachers now have to explain a toxic term like 'half-caste' to their classes.

Half-caste crunched:

[As this is a long poem we're going to apply a bigger cruncher and not necessarily choose words from each line]

EXCUSE - ONE - EXPLAIN - MEAN - PICASSO - CANVAS - HALF-CASTE - SKY - ENGLAND - OVERCAST - RASS - TCHAIKOVSKY - SYMPHONY - EXPLAIN - LISTENING - KEEN - UNDERSTAND - HALF-A-HAND - SLEEP - HALF-A-DREAM - HUMAN - MUST - WHOLE - MIND - OTHER - STORY

NB

Different readers will probably interpret the tone of Agard's poem differently. For some, the poem might sound aggressive, accusatory and confrontational. And sometimes it is necessary to be confrontational, when you're faced with injustice, prejudice and oppression, centuries of it, and when this injustice is embedded within a culture, its language and its behavioural norms. Agard's poem is a kind of protest song on behalf of a marginalised minority. Certainly, there's a steeliness and a directness to the poem and the poet is clearly angry about these issues. But, to me, this anger seems to be tempered by, and mixed in with, a winning sense of humour. We've already discussed the opening image. Add to that the description of English weather: Agard personifies English clouds as so 'half-caste' they are 'overcast' and as acting out of 'spite' against the sun. Moreover, the poet consistently makes the opposing views seem absurd, comically foolish. Sometimes humour is the most persuasive tactic. Finally, watch and listen to this irrepressibly expressive poet performing this poem and you can make up your own mind as to the tone and spirit *Half-Caste* should be read and received in: https://www.youtube.com/watch?v=zDQf2Wv2L3E

Dylan Thomas, *Do Not Go Gentle into that Good Night*

Thomas's poem is written in the first person, but the 'I' only comes in during the final stanza, when we realise that the poet has been addressing the poem specifically to his dying father: 'And you, my father, there on the sad height'. Having started with a seemingly generalised public imperative to people in old age, the poem circles towards this deeply personal finale. The withholding of the personal voice makes its eventual appearance in the poem more dramatic and powerful. Before the poet and his father come into it, the poem concerns itself with character types; wise men, good men, wild men, grave men, and the different reasons why they don't not go quietly to their deaths. These types give Thomas examples by which to measure the success of his father's life, and implicitly his own.

What do we learn of the characters of father and son? Well the son, the poet, is using this difficult villanelle form, its repeat lines and formality, to wrestle strong and potentially overwhelming emotions under control. But when we also know that the father was a teacher of English and lover of literature, we have a sense of a son wanting to please his father with an unassailably great poem, to prove his poetic mastery once and for all. Perhaps even to show off a bit. Look dad! Look what I've made! And of course, in the world of  the poem, the father's death, though impending, is always in the future, has never happened. So there is an element of the poet's wish-fulfilment. But also there is the sense of the poet bringing on the father's death – reading the poem you would have the impression the father's death was imminent.

The main verbs used by the narrator are: 'Do not go'; 'rage'; 'dying'; 'curse'; 'bless'; 'burn'. The repeat lines are imperatives, commands, instructions. The narrator's use of these imperatives in conjunction with the modal verb, 'should', imply that he is in command of the situation. However, the grammatical function of these words is undermined by their context. The rhetorical imperatives may sound superficially powerful, but the gap between the sound of the language and its ability to affect the father betrays the poet's lack of agency. In short, as the poem progresses the grammatical commands read as pleading.

Father & son

Thomas's father was an atheist, so that for him his impending death was very definitely the 'end'. The poem never contradicts this view; all the way through, death is described as the end. However, it is the first use of the words 'my father' which, ironically given this father's atheism, alerts us to some spiritual yearning in the poet. The little harmonic echo of meaning of 'priest' that comes with the word 'father' is confirmed in the next line, where the poet moves for the first time from a tone of apparent command to one of overt supplication:

'Curse, bless, me now with your fierce tears, I pray.'

In the second line we are told old age should 'burn' and 'rave'. Indirectly, these verbs reveal the feelings of the poet. He implores his father to fight hard against dying which suggests just how much he loves and fears losing him. The verbs associated with the old men, wise men and the other character types are: know; had forked; crying; danced; caught; sang; learn; grieved; see; blaze; be. The instructions are turned then to the poet's father: curse; bless. Then the repeat lines return at the end and are now directed in all their universality and power at the poet's dying father. But first the weight of the whole poem and its tone of command and instruction is modulated by the poet's only verb: *I pray.*

The sad height

According to the Chambers Dictionary, euphemism is 'a figure of rhetoric by which an unpleasant or offensive thing is designated by a milder term'. We tend to find euphemistic language is used around subjects which are in some way 'untouchable', or taboo. It is usually a means of evading, or glossing over, or just making light of realities that are hard to face directly. Naturally the older we get, the more attractive euphemistic language around death becomes. There are many euphemistic terms for death, such as 'passed away', 'at rest' and 'kicked the bucket'. Rather like dead metaphor [e.g. 'a chair leg'], euphemistic language often creeps by unnoticed. But if you listen out for it you will find it is widely used. You hear genocide referred to on the news as 'ethnic cleansing', and the inadvertent killing of civilians called 'collateral damage'. Or elderly relatives announcing that they are going to 'spend a penny'.

What possible use could a poet make of euphemism? Isn't it part of a poet's job to bring us closer to reality, not evade it, gloss over it, or distance us from it? Dylan Thomas makes euphemistic language central to this poem. We will see that it enables him to achieve the emotional distance required to deal with an ultra-taboo subject. But at the same time, something miraculous occurs; that same apparently emotionally distancing language also uncannily allows the reader closer to the reality he is describing. The first thing to note is that it always appears as a line ending. The two repeat lines or refrains both end with key euphemistic imagery; 'that good night' and 'the dying of the light'. The two other examples are end of line 2 'at close of day' and end line 16 'on the sad height'. 'At close of day' ties in with the age-old idea of death as a kind of sleep, e.g. 'And our little life is

rounded with a sleep' [from *The Tempest*]. It's implication of sunset and then darkness ties in with the rest of the poem's imagery of light for life, dark for death:

- 'lightning'
- 'bright' waves
- 'the sun'
- 'blaze like meteors'.

What makes this imagery of dynamic, burning light different and startling is that it is in the context of people realising late in life how much more light they could have had, how much more fully they could have lived, and being angry, raging about that fact.

Line 16 '...on the sad height' uses the metaphor of life as an ascent: old age is a plateau reached near the top of a mountain, where the ageing process all but ceases, there is a creeping but also climbing upwards towards death, until there really is nowhere else to go, except the ever so slightly higher summit, which is death. Time is passing, but less is happening. The phrase gives

us a sense of time for reflection, perhaps wisdom, greater insight, perhaps, but no more action.

As remarked earlier, euphemism is usually softens hard reality. It does so here too. As a result of the distancing euphemisms we don't feel mawkishly close to the death-bed, or feel that the poet is being self-indulgently emotional or self-pitying. But the use of this kind of language in both refrains has a strange effect. The repetition gives the reader a sense knocking on the doors of the exact meaning and imagery of each euphemism, trying to open it up, trying to get in. The poem won't permit us to let the euphemism glide by and have a numbing or pacifying effect. Instead it wakes up to its own effects through the course of the poem. Each time a line is resurrected we become more aware of it, and it more directly and intensely suggests death.

The poem is not just about death, it is about the impending death of the poet's father. This is what makes it really taboo - it is addressed to the poet's living father, regarding his impending death. In fact he lived for over a year longer.

A complex dance

The rhyme scheme is aba aba aba aba aba abaa. Being on only two rhymes makes the poem a closed form. This is accentuated by the two repeat lines, which each occur four times in the poem. In tension with this sealed closedness is the simultaneously expansive and commanding note struck by the repeat lines. Because they have to bear being repeated each line they need to be open in the sense that they can bear different weights and loads of meaning from the lines around them as the poem progresses. They sound rather cool and almost detached when we first hear them, but by the end those same lines are freighted up with grief and desperation.

The poet uses the technique of two verbs linked by 'and' to create a feeling of activity:

- 'burn and rave'

- 'caught and sang'.

This sense of poise and balance echoes the idea of hovering between life and death. The first line is an arresting and unusual construction: '<u>Do not</u>' sets the tone as formal and commanding from the off, and 'gentle' where we expect 'gently' brings the reader's mind to a slight pause and jarring appropriate for what follows – the poem's word order is at times used to slow the reader, reading the poem is intentionally a syntactically bumpy ride.

Thomas's poem is a technically complex, interlocking form called a villanelle. Written in three line, tercet, stanza form, a villanelle uses only two rhymes. The second lines of each tercet rhyme with each other and all the other lines rhyme together. Moving like figures in a complex formal dance, the first and third lines of the poem repeat alternately as the third lines in subsequent stanzas, and are finally recycled to make the very last two lines of the poem. A villanelle finishes with a shift in stanza form to a quatrain. In a great villanelle like this, repeated lines build in resonance and power as the poem progresses, and they blend in seamlessly with the surrounding lines. They make the poem's movement circling and wavelike rather than flat  and linear. Their statement and restatement gives a feeling of the provisional, but also can as here be used to capture desperation, anxiety and enclosure.

Notice too how each stanza ends with a full stop, completing one seemingly closed circuit. Only for this circuit to start up again in the proceeding tercet. Within each circuit there is also a distinct pattern in which power is generated then dissipated. This pattern is most distinct in the first stanza: Here the imperative tone of 'do not' and the vibrant, violent imagery contained in the commanding opening verbs 'burn', 'rave' and 'rage' give way to euphemistic language at the ends of the lines; 'good night', 'close of day' and 'dying of the light'. This semantic sense of a dying fall is re-enforced both sonically and metrically. In the final line, in particular, the harsh, guttural, assonantal first three words are bunched in heavy, emphatic stresses. The second half of the line, in contrast, opens up. Lighter stresses carry less sonically dense sounds, falling on the 'i' assonances:

Rage, **rag**e, **aga**inst the dying of the light
Tum   tum   ti tum   ti tum ti ti ti TUM

It would have been simplicity itself for Thomas to turn 'dying of the light' to the more concentrated 'rage, rage against the dying light'. The fact that he didn't signals that these weak, thin, unstressed function words perform an important sonic role.

Burning brightly

Dylan Thomas was a flamboyant Welsh poet famous for readings of his work. He wrote this poem in the Summer/Autumn of 1951. His father died in December 1952. Dylan Thomas's sister died of cancer in Bombay in April 1953. Having burnt brightly, Dylan Thomas himself died in November 1953, aged 39 years. Thomas embraced rhyme and often tackled difficult poetic forms. With a highly lyrical poetic style and famously lush orchestration of language he was at violent odds with the dominant poetic manner of his time. In particular, 'The Movement' poets, such as Philip Larkin, distrusted such high-blown rhetoric. Movement poets employing every day, colloquial diction to produce ironic reflections on the contemporary, modern world. Thomas's style, in comparison, is headier, richer, more incantatory and his subjects reach back into the Romantic. One of The Movement writers, Kingsley Amis, famously jibed about Thomas 'spewing words like beer'. Though he only ever wrote in English, Thomas's mother and father both knew the Welsh language. Perhaps the strict forms are to some extent a nod to the Welsh Bardic tradition, famous for its exacting technical rigours.

Do not go Gentle crunched:
NIGHT – AGE – RAGE – DARK – LIGHTNING – GENTLE – WAVE – DEEDS – DYING – SUN – GRIEVED – GOOD – BLINDING – BLAZE – LIGHT – FATHER – BLESS – GENTLE – RAGE

Christina Rossetti, *Remember*

Rossetti's poem, which opens 'Remember me when I am gone away', is oft-used at funerals. As such it has a cultural identity that aids its effectiveness in stirring sad emotions in us; joining other traditionally used elegies, it presents the speaker from beyond the grave as stoical, selfless and wise. Of course, the poem is spoken by someone living; yet the fact that it is most often used to give a voice to the dead means that it has taken on a different cultural legacy. Its immediate intelligibility lends itself to oral performance. We can hear it once and form a strong sense of its meaning. Rossetti uses very few obvious poetic flourishes or ornamentation; in keeping with the serious material and matter-of-fact tone, the language of *Remember* is unfussily modest and straightforward.

Rossetti was an English poet who belonged to a well-known group of artists and literary figures known as the Pre-Raphaelites. The Pre-Raphaelites sought to return to art as it was composed before or 'pre' the Italian artist Raphael. Specifically they wanted to revive the use of precise detail and intense colour pallets of 15th century Italian art. Christina Rossetti sat for some of the movement's well-known paintings, such as her brother Dante's *The Girlhood of Mary Virgin*.

Rossetti's most famous poem, *Goblin Market,* is full of dark and challenging subversions of the typical children's genre and has proved fertile ground for a host of theoretical excavations from feminists, psychoanalytical readers and Marxists. On the surface at least, *Remember* seems a less controversial, more conventional poem.

Remember x 4

The poem uses four 'remember's. The first two set up the command to remember, and the second two quantify these to re-iterate the need for the

reader not to forget the speaker of the poem, the person who has died/ will soon die. The first two 'remember's are imperatives, setting the tone for the sentence that will ensue. So is the third; 'and afterwards remember, do not grieve'. However, the last one is in a subordinate clause, linguistically softer, less firm. It is as if Rossetti uses the four markers to take the reader through the journey of grief; from denial and anger in the first part of the poem, with firm,
imperative language, to the sadness and acceptance of 'remember' being in the subordinate [or dependent clause].

The first two uses of the word also talk about the future, and the hope of what is lost; the 'silent land' of death is infinite, without the structure of the 'day by day'. Indeed, the poem is full of ambiguous time frames- 'a while', 'our future that you plann'd', 'the thoughts that once I had'. Is it as if the speaker is already occupying that space where time has stopped working. The tone of the poem finds its home in a half-existence that is only conjured into being by the implied consciousness of the speaker. The second half of the poem distances itself even further from the present- 'yet if you should forget me for a while / and afterwards remember'. The poem takes us from the first, raw hurt of grief through to future healing in the space of a sonnet's fourteen lines-perhaps it is this swift, but restrained outline of the process of grief that leads people to be so emotionally affected by it.

Sometimes saying less, but saying less precisely, can mean more than using lots of looser words. Characteristically Rossetti uses euphemism to underplay the suffering involved in this scenario, including her own. She describes her death, for instance, twice with the casual, everyday phrase, 'gone away'. And death itself is described only as a 'silent land'. The grim reaper is banished from the poem. Absence of the beloved is imagined as no longer being able to hold their hand. The only moment when the chasm of grief begins to open up and threaten to crack the verse's marble-like surface is in the ominous phrase 'darkness and corruption'.

The poem's understated language may be composed predominantly of ordinary words, but their intense patterning is rhetorical. Repetition is a particularly marked feature. Anadiplosis sounds like a long extinct dinosaur, but actually it's a term from rhetoric describing ending one line with a phrase and the using it at the start of the next line. Rossetti uses it with 'gone away / Gone far away'. Notice how the addition of the simple word 'far' adds emotional weight to the phrase. Other words and phrases repeated include 'no more', 'should', 'far', 'when' etc. Rhetoric, of course, is appropriate for a poem which seeks to persuade its reader of something. Rossetti's poem counsels the reader not to grieve. Subtextually, of course, it implies that they/ we must cherish the beloved while we can, before they leave us.

Naturally modern readers do not assume that male poets would be manly and resolute in attitude and matter-of-fact in style. Nor would we think men would especially demonstrate these qualities when facing a subject as grim as their own mortality. If we were tempted to make such gendered assumptions, many of the poems in this anthology would swiftly disabuse us. Equally, we would not expect female poets to be emotional in tone nor florid in expression. Nevertheless, it is striking how Rossetti radically reverses Victorian gender stereotypes and it would be interesting to see whether students would gender the poem as male or female if the writer's sex was withheld. *Remember* might not subvert convention as obviously as *Goblin Market*, but it does, in this way, overturn Victorian expectations. Perhaps too the poem's firmly buttoned-up emotion, its stiff-upperlipedness is also an essentially English characteristic. <u>Would the poem be more powerful if Rossetti released her emotions from all this restraint? Would we get something more American and, perhaps, something mawkish?</u>

Going down in good order

What's most striking about this poem is its control. Language is instrumentalised and employed with tremendous precision. There's not a touch of post-structuralist slipperiness to this language or any hint of what T.S. Eliot called the writer's 'intolerable wrestle with words'. Rossetti exerts mastery on her words and through them over her emotions. The management of structural aspects makes this most evident: syllables, the rhyme scheme, lineation, syntax and metre are all kept in good working order. For instance, each line is composed of exactly ten syllables, none are even one more or fewer. All the rhymes are also full and, despite the stringent technical challenges of the Petrarchan form with its limited number of rhyme sounds, the rhymes slide into place like parts of a well-oiled machine. Each of the first two quatrains is also composed of one sentence that completes itself neatly on the last word of each stanza. This repeated syntactical pattern also neatly brings the poem to the volta, after the octave, and the slight shift of focus in the sestet, signalled by 'yet'.

The metre too is a reliably regular iambic pentameter. Ticking over evenly, it keeps the underlying, potentially destabilising, emotions tucked away. Only on a couple of occasions can we hear small disturbances in the poem's even tread. Scan the lines and you'll notice only two slight deviations. The metrical wobbles occur in lines 3 and 12.

The first is a line composed entirely of monosyllables. A regular iambic pentameter would mean that the following syllables are emphasised:

'When **you** can **no** more **hold** me **by** the **hand**'.

Listen to the poem and the emphasis will, however, fall on 'more'. It's simply the more important word in the phrase 'no more' and the line invites a small pause before moving on to the verb 'hold'. Similarly, 'me' is surely more important in terms of semantics than the preposition 'by' and thus takes more emphasis. The alliteration of 'm' sounds further foregrounds these two words. The tension here between the poem's metrical pattern and its semantic and sonic ones generates this ruffling in the otherwise smooth surface.

In the second example, the regular metre would be: 'A **vest**ige **of** the **thoughts** that **once** I **had**', which would leave a clumsy and unnecessary stress on the small function word 'of'. Again, listen to the line and what we hear is more like 'A **vest**ige of the **thoughts** that **once** I **had'**. This is a technique known as pyrrhic substitution, where one stress is diminished, here 'of', so that the following one on 'thoughts' is strengthened. The metrical trailing off and then re-strengthening is highly appropriate to the sense of what is being said. Overall, the extraordinary control of the poem manifests over its material, the exertion of will and reason over destabilising emotions exemplifies, neatly, the poem's overt message to its reader.

How, though, is the reader to feel about being accused, potentially, of forgetting this speaker? Memory is a complicated thing because it calls into question what we call reality, and what we judge as being a real experience. The fact that this poem is culturally used most often to give voice to the dead [prosopopeia] as opposed to giving voice to those about to die means that there is a lack of ability for the reader to reply. Gently it may be, but the poem actually accuses the listener or reader of forgetting someone that they have lost- even the opening line wants to make the reader protest with something along the lines 'Of course I will!' The reader has no right of reply to these accusations, which means that they are left to examine and recognise their own shortcomings in relation to grief and moving on with their lives. There is a silence where there should be correspondence, or a counter-argument.

Because the reader has no opportunity to say that they will, of course, remember the person who has passed away, there is a double sadness to which people react: the sadness of the death and the guilt that they might one day fulfil the accusation of the poem. Narrative silences are important in literature because they indicate an inability to respond, and a conspicuous gap where there would otherwise be someone controlling the narrative. Interestingly, here it is the person who is either dead, or about to die, who has the voice; the person still living is made silent.

Do you think the poem would be more or less effective if it were a dialogue between two specified people?

Afterlife

The afterlife isn't exactly a bustling party here, or a vision of Bacchus handing out the wine on Mount Olympus. It's an euphemistically phrased 'silent land' which has none of the 'future that you plann'd'. Worse, as we've noted, it's full of 'darkness and corruption'. This is a living person describing the grave, not a voice describing heaven. It's interesting to point out that Rossetti rejected a fiancé because he turned back to the Catholic Church; she began to become interested in the Anglo-Catholic Oxford movement, becoming a woman of religious devotion. Five years before *Remember* was written [1862] she had had a religious crisis. It's striking, therefore, that death in this poem doesn't lead to resurrection in the life beyond. This could have been a point of consolation – I will be dead but will live on eternally in heaven – but this is not what Rossetti wishes to emphasise. Whilst the 'silent land' could at a stretch indicate the heaven of eternal rest [as put forth in the New Testament] it is a curious turn of phrase - to describe heaven as a sterile and 'dark' place is theologically dubious at best. It seems more likely that as a non-devotional poem, this work addresses the very real, frequent and everyday way of coping with the enormously high death rate in Victorian Britain. It has the tone of a didactic tale on how to cope with death.

There's an interesting dynamic in the fact that the speaker here effectively writes their own elegy. It's important to be aware of how we perceive control over a literary narrative- but even more here, the person about to die is trying to guide the memories that other people have of them, which form a sort of afterlife in themselves. It also creates and maintains the exact life after death which the speaker is arguing perhaps doesn't exist in the 'silent land'. Whenever the poem is read or spoken, this idea is continually recalled and comes to symbolise much bigger ideas of loss, grief and pain through Rossetti's unspecific and ambiguous terminology. She does not tie her speaker down to a time or a place; the lack of response from another voice means that the poem comes to represent all those who have passed away, and the slow transition of time that ensures an afterlife in memory, as well as a general fading of conscience.

Form and allusion

It's in the classic form of a Petrarchan sonnet, often used in poems where the subject is unrequited love. Normally, however, it is the speaker of the poem that is suffering from unrequited love; here it is the reader.

An allusion to the tale of Orpheus and Eurydice can be found in the line 'nor I half turn to go yet turning stay'. Orpheus, after the death of his beloved

Eurydice, goes down to Hades to ask for Eurydice back. Hades tells him that he can take her back to the living world on one condition; that on walking out of the Underworld, he should not look back at her, but instead carry on walking lest she be lost for ever. Obviously [because these things don't have happy endings] he turns around to see her because he lacks faith in what the gods have told him. The speaker of the poem wants the reader to have faith that they should be separated, and it is right and proper that this should happen; to chase the person who has died into the 'silent land', or Hades, is not what has been intended by fate. The same 'turning back' can also be found in the sestet, where the speaker describes 'Yet if you should forget me for a while / And afterwards remember, do not grieve'; it is implied that one turns back to grief as one turns back to a memory of a loved one.

Remember crunched:

REMEMBER – GONE – SILENT – HAND – STAY – REMEMBER – FUTURE – PRAY – FORGET – GRIEVE – DARKNESS – CORRUPTION – THOUGHTS – FORGET – SMILE – REMEMBER – SAD

Revision: Comparing the poems

The best way to explore relationships between these poems is, of course, to take a large piece of paper, write down all the titles and then use colours to make as many connections as you can between them. Connect them in terms of theme, form, language, images, perspective, rhymes and so forth. Remember to consider differences as well as similarities. Nuanced comparison also involves finding differences within superficial similarities and vice versa. What follows is a brief survey of possible comparisons. It is not intended to be comprehensive, but more a stimulus to your own thinking.

Mostly the poems in Edexcel's anthology fall into a number of groupings. The biggest of these are poems about childhood and growing up. Written in a first-person perspective, MacNeice's *Prayer Before Birth* obviously is set the earliest and conveys a disturbing image of a nightmarish world the innocent unborn child might enter. The child in Fanthorpe's *Half-past Two* has made it to primary school, but they also struggle to understand the adult world. Unlike, MacNeice's poem, however, though there is traumatic experience at the heart of *Half-past Two*, there's also a touch of gentle humour introduced primarily through the third person narrator's asides. Both poems also imagine a sanctuary, a space beyond or within their contexts in which the child can be safe and free. The relationship between a child and the wider world is also explored in Scannell's *Hide and Seek*. Like Fanthorpe in her poem, Scannell also tries to take us into the mind of a child, though the language in his poem is more grown-up. The voice in Kipling's *If* is distinctly adult, with the poem addressed to a child rather than being about childhood. Manliness is also in the background of Lawrence's *Piano* where childhood is associated with the security and comfort of home and overwhelming emotion appears to be emasculating.

Several poems explore loving relationships. Shakespeare's *Sonnet 116* is a famous love poem often used in marriage services. It seems unlikely that either Keats's or Browning's poems would be put to the same use, as both present darker aspects of love - obsession, bewitchment, jealousy, murder and so forth. Elizabeth Barrett Browning's sonnet, *Remember*, poignantly conveys feelings about the loss of love through the ultimate separation of lovers through death. Dylan Thomas's *Do Not Go Gentle into that Good Night* and Walker's *Poem at 39* explore loving relationships between children and parents and both poems are also shadowed by mortality. Using the strict closed form of the villanelle, Thomas conveys his anguish at the thought of his father's death, whereas Walker chooses a homelier style and free verse form to celebrate her father's life and the effect he has had on her own character.

Of the remaining poems, both *Search for My Tongue* and *Half-Caste* concern the nature of identity and more specifically how language shapes our sense of self. Both poems are written by writers who embrace a hybrid sense of identity and both also deviate from Standard English, although to different extents. Agard's poem, however, is addressed at imaginary listener, whereas Bhatt seems more addressed to herself. Written in the third person, Duffy's *War Photographer* also features a character out of sorts with a society which shows little appreciation for his work. Like Agard's and Bhatt's poems, Duffy's poem concerns the material out of which reality is constructed and represented, although in her poems it is images rather than words.

Dharker's and Blake's poems can both be read through either innocent or experienced perspectives and both arguably are concerned with religion. Blake's mesmeric tiger could also be compared with Keats's bewitching belle dame; both are strikingly beautiful, wild and exotic, but also destructive.

Checking the sample assessment materials provided by Edexcel reveals that their questions might not take a thematic approach in terms of linking poems, but use instead more general aspects. So, for instance, a sample question asks you to compare 'the ways' writers present powerful images in *Blessing* and *War Photographer*. Writing all the titles out on paper, making connections and, of course, writing practice essays will make you adept at this sort of exercise.

A sonnet of revision activities

1. Reverse millionaire: 10,000 points if students can guess the poem just from one word from it. You can vary the difficulty as much as you like. For example, 'mastery', from Lawrence's poem would be fairly easily identifiable whereas 'weep' would be more difficult. 1000 points if students can name the poem from a single phrase or image – 'portion out the stars and dates'. 100 points for a single line. 10 points for recognising the poem from a stanza. Play individually or in teams.

2. Research the poet. Find one sentence about them that you think sheds light on their poem in the anthology. Compare with your classmates. Or find a couple more lines or a stanza by a poet and see if others can recognise the writer from their lines.

3. Write a cento based on one or more of the poems. A cento is a poem constructed from lines from other poems. Difficult, creative, but also fun, perhaps.

4. Read 3 or 4 other poems by one of the poets. Write a pastiche. See if classmates can recognise the poet you're imitating.

5. Write the introduction for a critical guide on the poems aimed at next year's yr. 10 class.

6. Use the poet Glynn Maxwell's typology of poems to arrange the poems into separate groups. In his excellent book, *On Poetry*, Maxwell suggests poems have four dominant aspects, which he calls solar, lunar, musical and visual. A solar poem hits home, is immediately striking. A lunar poem, by contrast, is more mysterious and might not give up its meanings so easily. Ideally a lunar poem will haunt your imagination. Written mainly for the ear, a musical poem focuses on the sounds of language, rather than the meanings. Think of Lewis Carroll's

Jabberwocky. A visual poem is self-conscious about how it looks to the eye. Concrete poems are the ultimate visual poems. According to Maxwell, the very best poems are strong in each dimension. Try applying this test to each poem. Which ones come out on top?

7. Maxwell also recommends conceptualising the context in which the words of the poem are created or spoken. Which poems would suit being read around a camp fire? Which would be better declaimed from the top of a tall building? Which might you imagine on a stage? Which ones are more like conversation overheard? Which are the easiest and which the most difficult to place?

8. Mr Maxwell is a fund of interesting ideas. He suggests all poems dramatise a battle between the forces of whiteness and blackness, nothingness and somethingness, sound and silence, life and death. In each poem, what is the dynamic between whiteness and blackness? Which appears to have the upper hand?

9. Still thinking in terms of evaluation, consider the winnowing effect of time. Which of the modern poems do you think might be still read in 20, a 100 or 200 years? Why?

10. Give yourself only the first and last line of one of the poems. Without peeking at the original, try to fill in the middle. Easy level: write in prose. Expert level: attempt verse.

11. According to Russian Formalist critics, poetry performs a 'controlled explosion on ordinary language'. What evidence can you find in this selection of controlled linguistic detonations?

12. A famous musician once said that though he wasn't the best at playing all the notes, nobody played the silences better. In Japanese garden water features the sound of a water drop is designed to make us notice the silence around it. Try reading one of the poems in the light of these

comments, focusing on the use of white space, caesuras, punctuation – all the devices that create the silence on which the noise of the poem rests.

13. In *Notes on the Art of Poetry*, Dylan Thomas wrote that 'the best craftsmanship always leaves holes and gaps in the works of the poem so that something that is not in the poem can creep, crawl, flash or thunder in'. Examine a poem in the light of this comment, looking for its holes and gaps. If you discover these, what 'creeps', 'crawls' or 'flashes' in to fill them?

14. Different types of poems conceive the purpose of poetry differently. Broadly speaking Augustan poets of the eighteenth century aimed to impress their readers with the wit of their ideas and the elegance of the expression. In contrast, Romantic poets wished to move their readers' hearts. Characteristically Victorian poets aimed to teach the readers some kind of moral principle or example. Self-involved, avant-garde Modernists weren't overly bothered about finding, never mind pleasing, a general audience. What impact do the Edexcel anthology poems seek? Do they seek to amuse, appeal to the heart, teach us something? Are they like soliloquies – the overheard inner workings of thinking – or more like speeches or mini-plays? Try placing each poem somewhere on the following continuums. Then create a few continuums of your own. As ever, comparison with your classmates will prove illuminating.

Emotional..intellectual
Feelings..ideas
Internal..external
Contemplative..rhetorical
Open...guarded

Terminology task

The following is a list of poetry terminology and short definitions of the terms. Unfortunately, cruel, malicious individuals (i.e. us) have scrambled them up. Your task is to unscramble the list, matching each term to the correct definition. Good luck!

Term	Definition
Imagery	Vowel rhyme, e.g. 'bat' and 'lag'
Metre	An implicit comparison in which one thing is said to be another
Rhythm	
Simile	Description in poetry
Metaphor	A conventional metaphor, such as a 'dove' for peace
Symbol	A metrical foot comprising an unstressed followed by a stressed beat
Iambic	
Pentameter	A line with five beats
Enjambment	Description in poetry using metaphor, simile or personification
Caesura	
Dramatic monologue	A repeated pattern of ordered sound
Figurative imagery	An explicit comparison of two things, using 'like' or 'as'
Onomatopoeia	Words, or combinations of words, whose sounds mimic their meaning
Lyric	
Adjective	Words in a line starting with the same letter or sound
Alliteration	A strong break in a line, usually signalled by punctuation
Ballad	A regular pattern of beats in each line
Sonnet	A narrative poem with an alternating four and three beat line
Assonance	
Sensory imagery	A word that describes a noun
Quatrain	A 14-line poem following several possible rhyme schemes
Diction	When a sentence steps over the end of a line and continues into the next line or stanza
Personification	
	Description that uses the senses
	A four-line stanza
	Inanimate objects given human characteristics
	A poem written in the voice of a character
	A poem written in the first person, focusing on the emotional experience of the narrator
	A term to describe the vocabulary used in a poem.

GLOSSARY

ALLITERATION – the repetition of consonants at the start of neighbouring words in a line

ANAPAEST - a three beat pattern of syllables, unstress, unstress, stress. E.g. 'on the moon', 'to the coast', 'anapaest'

ANTITHESIS - the use of balanced opposites

APOSTROPHE – a figure of speech addressing a person, object or idea

ASSONANCE – vowel rhyme, e.g. sod and block

BLANK VERSE – unrhymed lines of iambic pentameter

BLAZON – a male lover describing the parts of his beloved

CADENCE – the rise of fall of sounds in a line of poetry

CAESURA – a distinct break in a poetic line, usually marked by punctuation

COMPLAINT – a type of love poem concerned with loss and mourning

CONCEIT – an extended metaphor

CONSONANCE – rhyme based on consonants only, e.g. book and back

COUPLET – a two-line stanza, conventionally rhyming

DACTYL – the reverse pattern to the anapaest; stress, unstress, unstress. E.g. 'Strong as a'

DRAMATIC MONOLOGUE – a poem written in the voice of a distinct character

ELEGY – a poem in mourning for someone dead

END-RHYME – rhyming words at the end of a line

END-STOPPED – the opposite of enjambment; i.e. when the sentence and the poetic line stop at the same point

ENJAMBMENT – where sentences run over the end of lines and stanzas

FIGURATIVE LANGUAGE – language that is not literal, but employs figures of speech, such as metaphor, simile and personification

FEMININE RHYME – a rhyme that ends with an unstressed syllable or unstressed syllables.

FREE VERSE – poetry without metre or a regular, set form

GOTHIC – a style of literature characterised by psychological horror, dark deeds and uncanny events

HEROIC COUPLETS – pairs of rhymed lines in iambic pentameter

HYPERBOLE – extreme exaggeration

IAMBIC – a metrical pattern of a weak followed by a strong stress, ti-TUM, like a heart beat

IMAGERY – the umbrella term for description in poetry. Sensory imagery refers to descriptions that appeal to sight, sound and so forth; figurative imagery refers to the use of devices such as metaphor, simile and personification

JUXTAPOSITION – two things placed together to create a stark contrast

LYRIC – an emotional, personal poem usually with a first-person speaker

MASCULINE RHYME – an end rhyme on a strong syllable

METAPHOR – an implicit comparison in which one thing is said to be another

METAPHYSICAL – a type of poetry characterised by wit and extended metaphors

METRE – the regular pattern organising sound and rhythm in a poem

MOTIF – a repeated image or pattern of language, often carrying thematic significance

OCTET OR OCTAVE – the opening eight lines of a sonnet

ONOMATOPOEIA – bang, crash, wallop

PENTAMETER – a poetic line consisting of five beats

PERSONIFICATION – giving human characteristics to inanimate things

PLOSIVE – a type of alliteration using 'p' and 'b' sounds

QUATRAIN – a four-line stanza

REFRAIN – a line or lines repeated like a chorus

ROMANTIC – A type of poetry characterised by a love of nature, by strong emotion and heightened tone

SESTET – the last six lines in a sonnet

SIMILE – an explicit comparison of two different things

SONNET – a form of poetry with fourteen lines and a variety of possible set rhyme patterns

SPONDEE – two strong stresses together in a line of poetry

STANZA – the technical name for a verse

SYMBOL – something that stands in for something else. Often a concrete representation of an idea.

SYNTAX – the word order in a sentence. doesn't Without sense English syntax make. Syntax is crucial to sense: For example, though it uses all the same words, 'the man eats the fish' is not the same as 'the fish eats the man'

TERCET – a three-line stanza

TETRAMETER – a line of poetry consisting of four beats

TROCHEE – the opposite of an iamb; stress, unstress, strong, weak.

VILLANELLE – a complex interlocking verse form in which lines are recycled

VOLTA – the 'turn' in a sonnet from the octave to the sestet

Recommended reading

Atherton, C. & Green, A. Teaching English Literature 16-19. NATE, 2013

Bate, J. Ted Hughes, The Unauthorised Life. William Collins, 2016

Bowen et al. The Art of Poetry, vol.1-12. Peripeteia Press, 2015-16

Brinton, I. Contemporary Poetry. CUP, 2009

Eagleton, T. How to Read a Poem. Wiley & Sons, 2006

Fry, S. The Ode Less Travelled. Arrow, 2007

Hamilton, I. & Noel-Todd, J. Oxford Companion to Modern Poetry, OUP, 2014

Heaney, S. The Government of the Tongue. Farrar, Straus & Giroux, 1976

Herbert, W. & Hollis, M. Strong Words. Bloodaxe, 2000

Howarth, P. The Cambridge Introduction to Modernist Poetry. CUP, 2012

Hurley, M. & O'Neill, M. Poetic Form, An Introduction. CUP, 2012

Meally, M. & Bowen, N. The Art of Writing English Literature Essays, Peripeteia Press, 2014

Maxwell, G. On Poetry. Oberon Masters, 2012

Padel, R. 52 Ways of Looking at a Poem. Vintage, 2004

Padel, R. The Poem and the Journey. Vintage, 2008

Paulin, T. The Secret Life of Poems. Faber & Faber, 2011

Schmidt, M. Lives of the Poets, Orion, 1998

Wolosky, S. The Art of Poetry: How to Read a Poem. OUP, 2008.

About the authors

Head of English and freelance writer, Neil Bowen has a Masters Degree in Literature & Education from Cambridge University and is a member of Ofqual's experts panel for English. He is the author of *The Art of Writing English Essays for GCSE*, co-author of *The Art of Writing English Essays for A-level and Beyond* and of *The Art of Poetry* series, volumes 1-14. Neil runs the peripeteia project, bridging the gap between A-level and degree level English courses: www.peripeteia.webs.com.

A secondary school English teacher in Hackney, Alice Penfold also works as an Examiner for A-Level and GCSE English and volunteers with the creative writing charity The Ministry of Stories. Prior to starting her teaching career, she worked in widening participation as a programme co-ordinator for the charity The Access Project and she maintains a long-term interest in educational equality and social mobility. Alice read English Literature at Oxford University.

Printed in Great Britain
by Amazon